African Intellectuals in the Post-colonial World

This book examines the role of African intellectuals in the years since the end of colonialism, studying the contribution that has been made by such individuals, both to political causes and to development within Africa.

Studying the concept of the "intellectual" within an African context, this book explores the responses of such individuals to crucial issues, such as cultural identity and knowledge production. The author argues that since the end of colonialism in Africa, various, often intertwining, factors, such as nationalism and co-option, have been used by black politicians or the political elites to muddle the roles and functions of black African intellectuals. Focusing on these confused roles and functions, the book posits that, over the years, most intellectuals in Africa have found the practice of "cheerleading" for a political cause more productive than making valuable contributions towards dynamic and progressive leadership in their countries.

This book will be of interest to students and scholars of African studies, politics, and development studies.

Fetson A. Kalua is a professor of English at the University of South Africa.

Routledge Contemporary Africa Series

Contesting Inequalities, Identities and Rights in Ethiopia
The Collision of Passions
Data D. Barata

Contested Criminalities in Zimbabwean Fiction
Tendai Mangena

Foreign Direct Investment in Large-Scale Agriculture in Africa
Economic, Social and Economic Sustainability in Ethiopia
Atkeyelsh G. M. Persson

Borders, Media Crossings and the Politics of Translation
The Gaze from Southern Africa
Pier Paolo Frassinelli

Life Writing from the Margins in Zimbabwe
Versions and Subversions of Crisis
Oliver Nyambi

Complex Adaptive Systems, Resilience and Security in Cameroon
Manu Lekunze

The International Criminal Court and the Lord's Resistance Army
Enduring Dilemmas of Transitional Justice
Joseph Otieno Wasonga

African Intellectuals in the Post-colonial World
Fetson A. Kalua

For more information about this series, please visit: www.routledge.com/
Routledge-Contemporary-Africa/book-series/RCAFR

African Intellectuals in the Post-colonial World

Fetson A. Kalua

LONDON AND NEW YORK

First published 2020
by Routledge
2 Park Square, Milton Park, Abingdon, Oxon OX14 4RN

and by Routledge
52 Vanderbilt Avenue, New York, NY 10017

Routledge is an imprint of the Taylor & Francis Group, an informa business

© 2020 Fetson A. Kalua

The right of Fetson A. Kalua to be identified as author of this work
has been asserted by him in accordance with sections 77 and 78 of the
Copyright, Designs and Patents Act 1988.

All rights reserved. No part of this book may be reprinted or reproduced or
utilised in any form or by any electronic, mechanical, or other means, now
known or hereafter invented, including photocopying and recording, or in
any information storage or retrieval system, without permission in writing
from the publishers.

Trademark notice: Product or corporate names may be trademarks or
registered trademarks, and are used only for identification and explanation
without intent to infringe.

British Library Cataloguing-in-Publication Data
A catalogue record for this book is available from the British Library

Library of Congress Cataloging-in-Publication Data
A catalog record for this book has been requested

ISBN: 978-0-367-26370-6 (hbk)
ISBN: 978-0-429-29524-9 (ebk)

Typeset in Times New Roman
by Apex CoVantage, LLC

Contents

Introduction   1

1   Theorising the concept of an intellectual   13

2   The "ivory tower" intellectual   30

3   The dilemmas of African intellectuals since the
end of colonialism: how modern African intellectuals
should steer clear of such sticking points   38

4   African intellectuals, culture, and decolonisation
of knowledge   50

5   Taking a leaf from the Western intellectual   65

6   A paradigm of an African intellectual in
the twenty-first century   75

Conclusion   87
Works cited   90
Index   93

Introduction

Preface

In this monograph, I make a case for how vitally important it is for the African continent to foster and promote opportune conditions for the development of intellectuals of all shades and stripes so that individuals of such calibre and endowment can help African countries to develop or attain the route to natural progression from largely backward to modern, advanced societies. Since the end of colonialism in Africa, so I argue, various, often intertwining, factors, such as nationalism, Pan-Africanism, and co-option, have been used by black politicians, or the ruling political elites, to muddle up and make a mess of the roles and functions of largely black African intellectuals. Thus, over the years, most black intellectuals in Africa have found the practice of cheerleading for a political cause more apt than making valuable contributions towards dynamic and progressive leadership in their countries. Surprisingly, for such intellectuals, the role they were expected to perform in their countries seemed to clash with the overall vision of independence from colonial rule, namely the cultivation of the kind of patriotism that was seen as being the only fitting approach to the issue of development. In other words, the ruling elites wanted everyone to have total faith in and harp on the themes of nationalism, which, as Tracy Fleming has argued, were

> simplistic perceptions of Black nationalism as unsophisticated appeals to group identity . . . rhetoric that is commonly marred by biological determinism, varying forms and articulations of xenophobia, and clearly undemocratic attitudes that are totally unrelated to solving social problems and addressing material conditions.
>
> (2016: 289)

2 Introduction

Such empty rhetoric by politicians partly explains the crisis of African intellectuals because, with some exceptions, quite a number of black African intellectuals are still seen as the type of intellectuals whose overriding task has been to cheerlead for either the notion of nationalism in general or personality cults in particular – all this in the name of nationalism or patriotism. For some reason, quite a number of black African political leaders who are, or have been, tyrants ensconced in power are, or have been, so cunning as to deflect some intellectuals' attention away from the key objective of bringing about substantive change and transformation in society. In order to co-opt intellectuals into politics, such politicians tend to hold out to such prospective intellectuals the carrot that power, as well as prestige, entails, thus smothering all the intellectual voices which society needs in order to be progressive. It is experiences such as these that inspired me to work on this monograph, which provides a platform for me to posit a paradigm for the kind of intellectuals the African continent needs in the twenty-first century.

Basically, throughout the monograph, I deal with and expound on the notion of the concept of the *intellectual*. As pointed out earlier, for a general understanding of the term, my use of the concept is not confined to the domain of the intelligentsia or university teachers. Rather, the concept of an intellectual ranges more widely to include varied roles that society's various individuals, who are deserving of the tag "intellectuals" in their own rights, can play to transform society through positive and constructive criticism. Thus, for a general understanding of the concept, initially, I offer a more inclusive and expansive definition of the word *intellectual*. Such an understanding is important in that one becomes familiar with different conceptualisations of the idea of an intellectual, seeing it as a wide-ranging and plastic concept which is about defining and characterising men and women of exemplary personality and attributes who are prepared to be custodians of people's rights and freedoms in society. In order to provide a wide perspective on the term, my use of the concept of *intellectual*, or *intellectuals*, is just as wide-ranging as some scholars have theorised and presented it. Hence, the concept is not confined to just academics, or scholars, whose main task is to teach in a university, where they are also expected to undertake research, but includes clever, intelligent, and gifted individuals who are often seen to be in the vanguard of all forms of change or transformation in society. To that end, I use the ideas of various scholars, notably Antonio Gramsci, Edward Said, Henry Goroux, Christopher Charle, Stefan Collini, Thomas Molnar, Noam Chomsky, and Julia Kristeva, to cite a few examples, who have theorised and presented the concept of an *intellectual* in various ways and from various perspectives. I broach and explicate the contentious subject or concept of an intellectual – a concept whose general sense, or understanding, has often seemed to point to the notion of the intelligentsia but whose semantic field is now so comprehensive and inclusive that it is no longer confined to the notion of the literati. Instead, the word *intellectual* now takes in any individuals who are actively and productively involved in public discourse and, for that reason, warrant the label intellectuals. Of course, a great deal has been written about this immensely interesting subject (of an *intellectual* or *intellectuals*), but I define, unpack, and contextualise the concept in the light of the global understanding and context of the term in general, and the African continent in particular.

How different is my approach?

I try to make a unique contribution to society by weighing in on the debate about the role of an African intellectual – an individual whose role should have a lasting impact on the future of the humanities in the world. This purpose was underscored in a report which was put together by both local and international reviewers of my research on the outcome of my application for rating with the National Research Foundation of South Africa (NRF) in 2015. Produced by international, as well as local, scholars, partly the report states that

> [t]he publication of a monograph based on your current research into the role of the public intellectual in Africa would augment your standing in the international community, and would enable you to contribute to the debate currently being conducted on the future of the humanities from the perspective of the global South.[1]

As far as writing a monograph is concerned, the preceding comments are instructive, as I hope it will be one of my major contributions to scholarship in the domain of the humanities, particularly with regard to the role of black African intellectuals in the changing world of the twenty-first century.

While various domains of extant knowledge, as well as the endless process of knowledge production itself, are key to all forms of transformation in society, they entail the involvement of clever and gifted people who have a deep and growing awareness of the currents of thought in such fields of knowledge. Strikingly, it is within domains of knowledge where notions of prejudice are played out because some of the knowledge is interpreted to suit particular groups of people, against others. Instances such as bias and prejudice do call for the role of an intellectual – a thinker whose engagement with either academic or public discourses makes him or her such a unique individual that she or he has the conscience and prudence to rise above any form of dualistic thinking which incites the spirit of partisanship.

4 *Introduction*

The definition of an intellectual in relation to Africa

As I have indicated, the senses in which I use the word *intellectual* in this monograph are based on the varied usage by various scholars. This is because there is a resurgence of interest in the hard realities of our time, notably transmogrifying modernities, globalisation, and technological advancement which make the concept, as well as the role, of an African intellectual, particularly a black one, somewhat extraneous to the demands of the twenty-first century. In other words, instead of grasping the nettle of the realities of modernity (the light of which shines in most post-colonial societies), globalisation, and technological progress, some black African intellectuals think of decolonising what they see as exclusively Western knowledge and resort to some fake reality of spurious unity on a continent of fractured identities which are often defined based on categories such as race, ethnicity, nationality, and religion, to use a few classifications. Further, to see a black African intellectual who is a member of the intelligentsia as the only figure who can solve Africa's problems is to take a somewhat limited, if not misguided, approach to the notion of an intellectual – a notion whose semantic field has now broadened to include various groups of people whose thinking, as well as acts of activism, can transform society. This is largely because, as far as Africa is concerned, through behavioural patterns such as co-option or whipping up politicians' sympathies, some black African intellectuals have contributed to ruining some African countries. In the meantime, those who choose to be genuine intellectuals are either chastised through incarceration or hounded out of their countries. In any case, since the end of colonialism, Africa remains the least developed and transformed landmass in the world. This is because of several factors, including political corruption, the fact that democracy has always been under strain, and that the continent is so rife with ethnic and religious tensions – all of which call for progressive intellectuals on the African continent who can transform society. In addition, Africa is still largely defined in terms of the prevalence of the triple ills of ignorance, disease, and hunger across the continent, meaning even though there are a great number of intellectuals in the domain of the intelligentsia, they have not made meaningful and substantial change to their societies. My argument is that the continent is largely underdeveloped since most black African "political" intellectuals who took over from traditional, pre-colonial ones, such as chiefs, do not actively play their roles of trying to transform their societies through active involvement in developing and shaping knowledge and public discourses.

Of course, it is worth stating the fact that, going back to the days of the colonial era, the African continent has always produced variegated types of pre-colonial intellectuals, notably traditional chiefs, some of whom kept the

Introduction 5

peace during the rise and fall of kingdoms. Then, since the time of colonialism to date, the types of black African intellectuals have ranged from those who interrogated and challenged the logic and praxis of colonialism through to the latter-day inspiring ones whose thinking is grounded on notions of universalism, notions that show what it means to be human. Such progressive intellectuals try to pinpoint and address issues of democracy, human rights, and various forms of freedoms. To that end, I broaden the universe of the discourse of intellectuals by addressing a range of questions, which include the following: Who or what is an intellectual? What is the intellectual's mission in society or life? What kind of black African intellectuals existed during Africa's pre-colonial past? How have black African intellectuals, particularly those who were linked with colonial discourse and feted for their remarkable contribution towards bringing the process of colonialism to its end, tried to cope with the dilemmas which have befallen post-colonial, post-independence societies with regard to issues such as political leadership, democracy, and human rights and the embrace of other freedoms in society? How have black African intellectuals dealt with the idea of culture in the aftermath of the colonial era? How do they respond to current discourses of decolonisation or decoloniality? Who is a typical African intellectual? What can African intellectuals learn from their Western counterparts? What paradigms of African intellectuals can inspire or help African political elites to steer clear of the vagaries of political leadership, culture, and tradition in the twenty-first century? Put another way, what kind of intellectuals should the African continent produce, largely through a good education, so that African societies have individuals whose objectivity and critical independence (through involvement in public discourses) is so exemplary that, rather than cheerlead for those in power, as well as for patriotism, they should help to transform societies? In short, there is a need to have African intellectuals as the kinds of individuals who are such dispassionate and unprejudiced thinkers that exist to transform their various societies across the African continent – societies whose major failings include a lack of democracy, as well as other freedoms which define for us what it means to be human.

Musings on the notion of an intellectual

The question of who an intellectual is is fully addressed in Chapter 1. As far as the meaning of the word *intellectual* is concerned, I can attest to the fact that a good number of people I have talked to have told me, albeit in the strictest confidence, that they find individuals called *intellectuals* somewhat boring, exhausting, unbearable, and unintelligible, to use a few terms which are often linked with this category of people.

6 *Introduction*

This is indeed surprising because, if such a general presupposition exists about intellectuals, then what type of individuals are these people who seem so uninteresting and well beyond anybody's understanding because they are generally wearisome or simply inarticulate and incomprehensible? Presumably, this is a category of individuals whom famous scholar Edward Said has portrayed as instantly recognisable in that they have the presumptions of being perceived as "super-gifted and morally endowed philosopher-kings"(1994: 6). In other words, these are individuals whose defining and enduring attributes are what Said has portrayed as "totally disengaged, otherworldly, ivory-towered thinkers, intensely private and devoted to abstruse, and perhaps even occult subjects" (ibid: 6). Here, Said refers to the kind of individuals whose Olympian detachment from society makes them so disengaged and highly quixotic in the way they go about their business that whatever they are involved in hardly benefits society. It must be said that such a delineation, at once fulsome and unflattering, is an unmistakable reference to academics, or individuals who are referred to as "ivory tower" intellectuals – persons who tend to incur and arouse the ire of either fellow intellectuals or the general public largely for being vainglorious, particularly when they use impenetrable language and pretentious diction. In other words, they tend to use the kind of language which leaves some people either at a loss or simply annoyed, precisely because they find themselves having to grapple with the type of language which merely draws attention to the pretentions of such a class of individuals called intellectuals. In this monograph, my use of the concept of *intellectual* includes but also largely exceeds the preceding delineation, which is an exclusive reference to individuals who work in academia. In short, I use the word *intellectual* in the widest possible sense to make reference to, and include, not only groups of individuals such as academics, but also non-academic though well-educated and enlightened members of society. These are a type of people who are such independent thinkers that, feeling conflicted about how particular issues are handled in society, try to deal with and speak out against such issues which impact on ordinary people's lives. Thus, my use of the word intellectual reflects its different senses. To that end, I explore all the fine and subtle distinctions between intellectuals of various shades and hues. In other words, throughout the monograph, I present and discuss gradations of the concept of an *intellectual* in an attempt to determine how intellectuals are identified, defined, and characterised in society. In doing so, I endeavour to expound on all the subtle distinctions which predictably emerge from the various connotations of the word *intellectual*, demonstrating the extent to which this concept may well be a trans-historical notion, and thus society has always had intellectuals of various shades and dispositions through the centuries.

Introduction 7

As for future African intellectuals, I consider, explore, and contextualise the notion and functions of a committed African public intellectual, with a view to mapping out a paradigm for the type of personality, as well as role, such an individual would be expected to perform on a continent that has now become part of the world which one would characterise as a cosmic bubble – a global society of promising prosperity and progress for all. In general, I use the word *intellectual* to denote an enlightened and well-informed individual – be it a university lecturer, schoolteacher, lawyer, judge, historian, journalist, or philosopher, to mention a few examples, who enters public life and is able to make independent judgements which help to shape the political and moral consciousness of the people. My argument is that, as far as a miscellany of issues such as race, gender, sexuality, ethnicity, religion, politics, and democracy are concerned, intellectuals should be seen as a bastion of all kinds of knowledge and freedoms in society as these individuals deal with such issues with critical detachment. Thus intellectuals are a beacon of hope for the people because, as great thinkers, they are self-appointed custodians of public morals and freedoms. Falling into Edward's Said's category of "organic" intellectuals, an intellectual understood in this sense is the kind of individual who tries to heighten public awareness about issues which relate to governance and life in general and which affect every individual in his or her day-to-day narrative of existences. This is particularly important because experience has shown that countries that are vibrant and attuned to human rights values, as well as the ideals of democratic principles, have allowed their "organic" intellectuals to take their place in society by ensuring that each one of such individuals is the type of personality

> whose whole being is staked on a critical sense, a sense of being unwilling to accept easy formulas, or ready-made clichés, or the smooth, ever-so-accommodating confirmations of what the powerful or conventional have to say, and what they do. Not just passively unwillingly, actively willing to say so in public.
>
> (Said 2003: 387)

Here, Edward Said underscores the function of an intellectual – an individual who is objective and broad-minded enough to ask challenging questions which relate to what are seen as conventional and normative ways of life. Such an individual ought to be fully involved and engaged in the affairs of his or her society by not just examining but also interrogating untested propositions, maxims, systems, and related ways of doing things, in order "to advance human freedom and knowledge" (ibid: 385). Further, in view of the cataclysmically dire situations in most black African societies, notably ethnic tensions and wars, I contextualise the idea of intellectuals in

8 Introduction

post-colonial and post-independence Africa in order to have an understanding of how engaged and productive some intellectuals are in their societies. At the same time, barring a few exceptions, I also demonstrate the extent to which some post-colonial and post-independence black African intellectuals were or have been conflicted about their roles in society by yielding to the lures of patriotism and co-option. For all sorts of reasons and considerations which range from fear of persecution by the ruling elites and opportunism to just the choice to remain indifferent to what is and has been going on in post-colonial societies, I demonstrate how such intellectuals have played the negative role of cheerleading for issues such as nativism, nationalism, and personality cults within the political arena, rather than their role as independent philosophers or thinkers. Such intellectuals have done this by either demonstrating their spirit of opportunism or parading the propensity for total indifference to what goes on in their societies. Thus, it is important to note that, in this monograph, I make a case for how important it is for the African continent to have intellectuals of all shades and hues – critical and conscientious thinkers who are primed with the right intellectual skills of objectivity and critical independence in order to help their societies to develop. Drawing on some examples, such as political, literary, and other figures, I try to show how various, often intertwining, factors such as colonialism, nationalism, and co-option have been used by the political elites to muddle up the roles and functions of most black African intellectuals. Thus, effectively, most intellectuals found the practice of cheerleading for a political cause more apt than contributing towards dynamic and progressive leadership in their various countries. For such intellectuals, the roles they were expected to perform seemed to clash with the overall vision and spirit of independence from colonial rule, namely the cultivation of the kind of patriotism which they saw as being germane to development. This explains why quite a number of intellectuals were seen cheerleading for either the notion of nationalism or personality cults, mostly in the name of patriotism. For some reason, quite a number of tyrants who found themselves ensconced in power were cunning enough to deflect some independent intellectuals' attention away from the key objective of bringing about substantive change and transformation in society. Such tyrants did so by either holding out the carrot that power or prestige entails or hounding libertarian and non-partisan intellectuals into exile. For example, independent-minded intellectuals and highbrow thinkers, notably Wole Soyinka and many good writers of fiction who were prepared to "speak the truth to power", to use Edward Said's expression, were either incarcerated or hounded into exile by their governments.

The first main theme I deal with is to expound on the notion of the intellectual. As pointed out earlier with regard to the general delineation of the concept

Introduction 9

of an intellectual, for a general understanding of the term, the concept of an intellectual is not confined to the intelligentsia or university teachers but ranges more widely to include individuals who have developed a deep awareness, or understanding, of the nature of knowledge and, hence, play various roles in society in order to drive the world forward. Thus, initially, a more inclusive and expansive definition of the word *intellectual* is offered for a general understanding of the concept. Such an understanding is important in that one becomes familiar with different conceptualisations of the idea of an intellectual, seeing it as a wide-ranging and plastic concept. In order to provide a wide perspective on the term, my use of the concept of intellectual is just as wide-ranging as some scholars have theorised and presented it. Hence, the concept of the intellectual is not confined to just academics or scholars whose main task is to teach in a university where they are also expected to undertake research.

The second major theme I deal with is about contextualising the idea of an intellectual in post-colonial, post-independence Africa. I argue that an intellectual is better placed to give voice to the march of events in society, especially with respect to issues such as ideologies, governance, culture, human rights, freedoms, and other related ideas. As Noam Chomsky has put it, "it is the responsibility of intellectuals to speak the truth and expose lies" (1967: 2). Chomsky's observation is interesting in that, as far as the issue of governance is concerned, there is a tendency of obfuscation and distortion in political circles, as well as in public life, by politicians and people whose major interest is power. Thus, it is the duty of the "organic" intellectual to conscientise the public about things such as political transgressions or wrongdoings, which are usually committed by those who wield power in society. Throughout the monograph, I demonstrate the extent to which the role of typically engaged African intellectuals, in whatever field, should be so clearly defined as to make them up-to-date with and attuned to what is happening in their societies.

The third theme I explore is about African intellectuals. As will become clear in this monograph, the concept of an African intellectual embraces a broad spectrum of individuals in society who are critical and independent thinkers and so engaged and fairly well-informed human beings on a range of issues and discourses which matter to society. Thus the idea of an African intellectual exceeds the notion of race, in this case the black African race. For example, born in Kenya, the late famous intellectual Ali Mazrui was of Indian descent. Further, during the apartheid era in South Africa, a great number of writers of fiction who destabilised the system of apartheid were white men and women. These individuals' unstated, paramount role was to mediate in and transform public discourses in ways which were perceived as notable humanistic interventions in the way that the South African society was supposed to function. Thus, I place a great deal of emphasis on the role of what Edward Said has termed "organic" intellectuals. Even if such

10 *Introduction*

an individual is a white, black, Indian, or Arab African, the most important thing is to be shaped by the African experience, meaning the knowledge and familiarity of living on the African continent. What such individuals have in common is their good and fully rounded education, which gives them an independence of mind to debunk human pretensions in politics, question certainties, and refuse to cave in to particular political habits of thought that make a fetish of dogmas and related philosophies that tend to reify ideology and related forms of orthodoxy at the expense of people's rights and freedoms. Individuals of this class are at the forefront of framing public opinion and are thus the very final bulwark against tyranny, oppression, and other excesses in society.

My attempt to clarify the notion of intellectualism in general and contextualise the idea of an African intellectual, in particular, is in order to pinpoint the role of an intellectual in post-colonial, post-independence Africa. Such an analysis might have a lasting impact on the future of the humanities on the continent and in the world. As the reader will become aware, the scope of the monograph is ipso-facto inter- and multi-disciplinary, with examples being drawn from disciplines such as history, politics, sociology, philosophy, and literature. It is hoped that the monograph will transform the intellectual field of study and reflection in Africa, where the concept of an *intellectual* is still largely linked with the notion of the intelligentsia. As I make clear throughout the monograph, the meaning of the word *intellectual* is imprecise, or indefinite, with its ambiguity and vagueness arising from the fact that society happens to abound with thinkers, mentors, and philosophers of various types and dispositions, all of whom are either deserving of or have always been associated with the designation *intellectual*. In general, and at a very basic and elemental level of conceptualising and understanding the notion of an intellectual, persons like teachers and priests – people who work in the domain of knowledge and culture and serve the general social interest in society – have been linked to the label intellectual. In this context, the term *intellectual* has other connotations which point to a unique group of people in society, such as teachers, lawyers, or academics with specialised skills. Thus, before contextualising the idea of the intellectual disposition which one would like to see reflected in the twenty-first century black African intellectual, I discuss the concept of an intellectual by using a holistic, all-inclusive approach – one which does not confine the term to university teachers or members of the intelligentsia but ranges more widely to include varied roles that society's various individuals who warrant the tag "intellectuals in their own right" can play.

In Chapter 1, I examine the idea of an intellectual by unpacking the term to reveal its broad-based, multiple, contrasting, and intersecting meanings. To that end, I use the ideas of various scholars, notably Antonio Gramsci,

Introduction 11

Edward Said, Henry Goroux, Stefan Collini, Thomas Molnar, Christopher Charle, Noam Chomsky, and Julia Kristeva, to use a few examples, who have theorised the concept of an intellectual in various ways. What comes out as self-evident is the fact that intellectuals are thinkers of various shades and dispositions. However, the core of intellectual enterprise is the spirit of objectivity, broadmindedness, critical independence, disinterestedness, and impartiality. These are intellectuals' valuable attributes, as they are useful when they deal with issues such as democracy, human rights, and various forms of freedom which are worth promoting in any society. Chapter 2 looks at "ivory tower" intellectuals – the category of thinkers who are conventionally perceived and understood as authentic intellectuals primarily because of their involvement with knowledge production in the academe. This largely conventional idea of an intellectual as a scholar who possesses the kind of expertise that enables him or her to teach and undertake research in a university or related institutions of higher learning is fully explored. My argument is that because of their specialised knowledge, such ivory tower intellectuals are also the type of individuals who should always try to be at the forefront of helping civil society to cultivate the kind of critical consciousness which paves the way for real change or transformation in society. Ivory tower intellectuals should make every effort to remain "organic" intellectuals by ensuring that they are visible and available for crucial interventions in society through their active involvement in and shaping of public discourse. Apart from publishing their works in scholarly books and journals, these intellectuals should also endeavour to pitch their works at levels which are accessible and available to the wider public. Further, besides scholarly works, these intellectuals should ensure that they participate in useful debates which provide a springboard for change in society. Chapter 3 discusses the so-called African intellectual – someone whose disposition has always shifted with the changing times, from pre-colonial through colonial to post-colonial times, and hence the dilemmas she or he has encountered in the process, including co-option and cheerleading for those in power. I show how modern African intellectuals should try to surpass particular kinds of predicaments, notably co-option, which their predecessors used to yield to. Chapter 4 considers the way in which an African intellectual has faced and dealt with the crucial issues of cultural identity and knowledge since the end of colonialism. In this case, what one finds worth decrying is African intellectuals' proclivity and partiality for ethnic and national cultures, even at a time when we live in a multi-cultural world. Such an alignment with culture is rather surprising given that, as far as the idea of culture is concerned, the peoples of Africa are as different as chalk and cheese. The chapter also looks at how African intellectuals should deal with the notion of decolonisation, or decoloniality. Chapter 5 is an analysis of the kind of intellectuals the

12 *Introduction*

Western world has produced in the last one hundred years or so with a view to garnering some salutary lessons from the way such intellectuals carried out their functions. Granted, Western intellectuals have had their own dilemmas, but at the same time, the West has produced some intellectuals who were great thinkers and whose positive and profound impact has been felt globally. The chapter shows what black African intellectuals can learn from such renowned Western ones. Finally, in Chapter 6, I provide the context of the rapidly changing world of the twenty-first century and hence argue for the kind of engaged intellectual whose knowledge is at the service of humanity. A great emphasis is placed on trying to proffer examples of both black and white African intellectuals who have initiated change or sweeping reforms in their societies.

Note

1 National Research Foundation of South Africa (2015).

1 Theorising the concept of an intellectual

What or who is an intellectual?

The question of who an intellectual is has been a complex subject for a long time. In a determined effort to define, contextualise, expound on, and provide an overview of the notion of the intellectual, it is the logic of Stephan Collini which instantly strikes one in that the idea of an intellectual has both an expansive definition and a broad application. As he has put it, the word *intellectual*

> is a term with a complex history, and many of the various senses and resonances deposited by that history are still active in the semantic field constituted by contemporary uses of the word.
>
> (2006: 15)

Such a reading of the term *intellectual* is interesting because, rather than the meaning of the word being a delimited one which is confined to a particular field of study, it is grounded on and open to various understandings and assumptions – the kind of assumptions which entail that the meaning of the concept goes beyond any distinctive, circumscribed, and specified definition. Clearly, the word's semantic field is a broad-based one. Hence, apart from the conventional understanding of the term to mean an academic or scholar, it is quite clear that history has bequeathed different shades of meaning to the word or concept of an *intellectual*.

In his further delineation of the term *intellectual*, Collini states that, because of its wide-ranging semantic field, the term

> refers to a type of person who acts in certain specific ways; and that therefore the question of determining whether or not this type of person exists or existed in various societies is . . . a matter of relatively unproblematic empirical investigation.
>
> (ibid: 15)

14 *Theorising the concept of an intellectual*

In other words, an intellectual is either a thinker who carries out a specific task or an advocate of some important vision or rights in society. Collini goes on to state that there is no "stipulative definition" (ibid: 46) of the word *intellectual*; hence, a person known as an intellectual "takes a committed interest in the validity and truth of ideas" (ibid: 46). In short, an intellectual is someone who is a savant in a particular domain of knowledge and, hence, has the confidence of his or her own people as she or he goes about the task of demonstrating what a commanding voice she or he has in a particular field of knowledge. Put another way, such a person could be involved in any kind of service, career, or vocation. The fact is that the defining and distinguishing nature of such an individual is that she or he carries out his or her duties in such a way as to bring about the force and agency of the various ideas in the realm of knowledge he or she is involved in so as to help society.

Yet again, Collin argues that the category of intellectuals

> tries to discriminate those whose occupations involve a *primary* involvement with ideas or culture from those whose orientation and purpose are directly practical: thus it will tend to include, say, journalists and teachers, just as it will tend to exclude, say, businessmen as well as manual workers.

(ibid: 46)

What is interesting is the fact that Collini sees the idea of an intellectual as one whose meaning has become fluid and shifting in that it pinpoints and identifies particular groups of people in society, against others, whose unique vocation concerns the need to grapple with problems whose solutions are not self-evident. In other words, the word *intellectual* is a term which is applied to many individuals in society whose inclination and abilities are not confined to the conventional idea of an intellectual as referring to a member of the intelligentsia.

One other scholar who has demonstrated great reflection on the idea of intellectuals is Thomas Molnar for whom "intellectuals . . . are the products of the Renaissance period" (1994: 20), and the emergence of this category of people "coincided with the initial stages of the transformations of Utopia into reality" (ibid: 20). Put another way, the idea of utopia had been used to refer to the medieval era which bore the hallmarks of the Christian faith of just the Roman Catholic Church mould. Thus, what reflected the idea of utopia during the medieval period was the ideology of the Christian faith. For Molnar, as the medieval society and era began to come apart, or disintegrate, it was the advent of the Renaissance period which ignited within some individuals the desire to go about their business like intellectuals so they could effect change in their society. This explains why Molnar states

Theorising the concept of an intellectual 15

that "we may not speak of 'intellectuals' in the early Middle Ages (until the twelfth century), and can hardly speak of them in any previous age" (ibid: 9). This is because, for him, it was the Renaissance period which engendered the emergence of intellectuals, most of whom were either scientists or those who introduced the idea of the Reformation in the sixteenth century in an attempt to reconstitute the Christian church, which was the Roman Catholic church. Thus, apart from scientists, other intellectuals were those individuals who wanted to move the religious worldview from Catholicism towards Pentecostalism. Further, Molnar asserts that

> an intellectual cannot be measured by his mental powers, insights, and creativity alone. It is, rather, the social milieu of which he is part, and the nature of his relationship to this milieu, that determine his role and status as an intellectual. In order to speak of "intellectuals", therefore, those who belong to this category must possess some degree of common consciousness of their role, their place in society, their relationship to those who are in power, and to those who seek it. In short, intellectuals form a *class* not by virtue of their organization, but to the extent that they have similar aspirations and influence, and a chance to be heard.
>
> (ibid: 9)

In other words, it takes more than brains for someone to become an intellectual as, in addition to cognitive and rational abilities, which are linked to the idea of an intellectual, such an individual should also use such competences as growing involvement in the community in order to help society to change and move with the times. An intellectual is someone who has a clear awareness of his or her role in society, particularly with regard to those who wield power.

In a different context, for Christophe Charle, "the most direct ancestor of the *intellectuel* was the *philosophe*, or 'a man of letters' of the eighteenth century" (2015: 12). The core of what Charle means here is that the precursor to the current concept of the intellectual was "a man of letters", or a highly knowledgeable person. He goes on to state that the idea of " 'a man of letters' had a much broader sense than it has today and included not just 'literary' writers but also philosophers and scientists" (ibid: 12) and that such an individual was "defined in opposition to the decadent academics stuck in their jargon" (ibid: 12). This is instructive in the sense that, even though Charle points to the eighteenth century as the time when intellectuals materialised, interestingly, the aforementioned attributes (of an intellectual) point to the fact that intellectuals have existed down the centuries. Also known as "a man of letters", an intellectual was either a writer of fiction, a philosopher, or a scientist. Thus an academic, as we understand the term,

16 *Theorising the concept of an intellectual*

was outside the realm of the concept of an intellectual. As far as the origin of the concept of an *intellectual* is concerned, Charle argues that "whereas earlier studies have always seen it as a transhistorical ideal" (ibid: 46), the "social figure of an *intellectuel* could appeal to an old tradition, that of the philosopher, the romantic poet, the artist 'for art's sake', and more recently that of the scientist" (ibid: 7). In other words, in order for one to have a full grasp of the idea of an intellectual, it is crucially important for one to examine the history of ideas. It is quite evident that the idea of an intellectual is a trans-historical reality, with different intellectual traditions with regard to definitions, attitudes to them, and other related factors as the shifting variants of the idea. Thus, even though the antecedent of the idea of an intellectual was a philosopher, this meaning shifted to refer to other thinkers, notably writers of fiction and scientists, who are located in various forms of knowledge.

Charle's conception and presentation of the concept of an intellectual is a compelling formulation, as it evokes and points to this notion as being a trans-historical one. In other words, the domain of knowledge known as intellectuals has existed since the dawn of time, and so it is plausible to reflect on different kinds of intellectuals throughout history or human existence. Thus, on reflection, and going back to the ancient Greeks, Socrates was a Greek philosopher who is famous for having come up with Socratic dialogue, which was about rhetorical examinations of any idea with a view to arriving at the truth. Thus, it is not surprising that, in order to arrive at the truth on any issue, Socrates used to ask probing questions and get people to come up with various responses to a particular, universal question until a consensus was reached with regard to various answers. To that end, Socrates was a powerful Greek intellectual. Plato was another philosopher of ancient Greece who conceived the idea of a hypothetical republic in which, so he argued, only philosophers could be the rulers because he believed that only a philosopher is a savant. Thus, in Plato's ideal republic, only philosopher kings would be the rulers. This is why Plato decided that in such a republic, poets should be banned because it could "damage the minds of the audience" (1974: 240) as poets as were seen as mere imitators whose work could cause unnecessary emotions in the audience. This explains why Emil Reich has described Plato as having been "certainly one of the best minds of the world" (1969: 1) because his criticism always bore "directly on the intellectual and emotional machinery of mankind" (ibid: 2). Further, as presented in the Bible, the first century AD saw the Pharisees as exceptional thinkers, or intellectuals, with regard to their fine grasp of the religious universe which defined their Semitic history and society because they were knowledgeable about Judaic laws and tradition. But, remarkably, it was Jesus Christ who emerged as the intellectual with

Theorising the concept of an intellectual   17

a most pragmatic approach to perceiving truth and reality. Whether seen from a religious or secular perspective, Jesus demonstrated his practicality as a typical intellectual in many ways. For instance, while the Pharisees' approach to the day of Sabbath was a rigid one, Jesus's approach to the issue was such a flexible one it made sense to state that the Sabbath was made for man and not man for the Sabbath. Further, Jesus paraded his pragmatism as an intellectual through his teaching by means of parables. For example, in his famous parable of the Good Samaritan, he demonstrated the importance of perceiving human identity by reminding the Jews to accept gentiles, or the idea of Otherness or difference. Fourthly, during the Middle Ages, or the medieval era, monks and friars were regarded as a type of intellectual as far as understanding life in terms of the religious world view of the time was concerned. In other words, it was the monks and friars who always taught the people what the worldview of their time was like. Fifthly, during the Renaissance period, the domain of intellectuals was defined first by the rise of science and later those who were involved in the process of the Reformation. Finally, during the period of Enlightenment, intellectuals were those individuals who were at the forefront of the discourse of modernity – "a period after the decline of feudalism in which we see the rise of secular science, technology, and rational philosophy" (Castle 2007: 317). A number of intellectuals would rise to question the idea of race, which was at the core of the notion of modernity – the notion which largely justified the idea of colonialism.

Probably the most influential intellectual to have emerged in the Western world in the first half of the twentieth century was a French philosopher by the name of Julien Benda. Although Benda was a philosopher, he was an intellectual par excellence and, hence, made an immensely positive contribution towards notions of politics and governance. For Benda, intellectuals are

> that class of men whom I shall designate "*the clerks*", by which I mean all those whose activity essentially is *not* the pursuit of practical aims, all those who seek their joy in the practice of an art or a science, or metaphysical speculation, in short in the possession of non-material advantages. . . . Indeed, throughout history, . . . I see an uninterrupted series of philosophers, men of religion, men of literature, artists, men of learning. . ., whose influence, whose life were in direct opposition to the realism of the multitudes.
>
> (1955: 30)[1]

As an avowed humanist himself, Benda's delineation of the word *intellectuals*, whom he gave the label *clerk*s, might sound idealistic, or impracticable, remains probably the most profound and insightful theoretical formulation

18   *Theorising the concept of an intellectual*

in that his model of intellectuals represents the kinds of individuals who make up the voice of reason, or the conscience, of humankind. Benda sees intellectuals as "men of religion, men of literature, artists, and men of learning" whose overriding aims in their lives are "in direct opposition to the realism of the multitudes". In short, there are various groups of individuals in society who comprise, reflect, and evince the notion of an intellectual by challenging certain forms of knowledge which are taken for granted. For Benda, at the core of the idea of an intellectual is the fact that she or he is a disinterested thinker who spends time reflecting on issues which affect society, ensuring that she or he fulfills her or his obligation of standing for justice and truth at all costs, even if the consequences of such actions may lead to her or his death by those in power. Benda's approach points to the fact that he is a firm believer in universal and eternal values which intellectuals should promote, as they are a constant reminder of what it means to be human. For Benda, on one level, an intellectual is almost a Socratic philosopher king – a man or woman of some learning who is indispensable to the running of the state because of the skills she or he has. It is clear that Benda's model of intellectuals represents those individuals who devote their lives to the kinds of causes which are meant to nourish the mind, as well as the soul. This explains why some of the examples Benda gives as his type of intellectuals are people such as men of the cloth, academics, and artists, including musicians and writers of fiction. Interestingly, like Benda, Henry Girouw has also defined a public intellectual as someone who belongs in the category of individuals including "artists, journalists, academics, and others who have been innovative and daring, willing to challenge the conventions of the dominant political and social order" (2002: 383). In short, both Benda and Girouw provide a wide-ranging and compelling framework of who an intellectual is or what he or she should be like. What emerges from the various elaborations is the fact that an intellectual is a well-informed individual who inhabits a privileged space in a social group or society, in that she or he has a clear sense of direction, as well as possessing particular skills and ample critical independence to be able to lead and meaningfully engage in discourses which matter and contribute towards society's transformation. Unsurprisingly, Benda's approach to thinking about the concept of an intellectual would be used or adapted by later scholars, notably Antonio Gramsci and Edward Said.

In the second part of the twentieth century, Europe saw the emergence of various scholars who would build on the work by Julien Benda with regard to notions of what or who an intellectual is. One such scholar was a famous Marxist scholar, Antonio Gramsci, who also provides comprehensive and particularly illuminating insights into the notion of who an intellectual is, as well as spelling out what special functions such an individual is expected

Theorising the concept of an intellectual   19

to perform in society. Writing in an essay entitled "The Intellectuals" (from "Prison Notebooks"), Gramsci delimits the concept of an intellectual in a way which renders visible the certainty of the existence of intellectuals of different shades and hues in every community or society. Presumably, drawing on Julien Benda's ideas, he defines an intellectual broadly as "an organizer of society in general" (Gramsci 1996: 184). For Gramsci, just like Benda before him, intellectuals are to be understood in terms of their social function. They are mandarins, or pundits, of lateral thinking – a vital dimension of creative and imaginative reasoning which is key to addressing problems in society. Hence, as persons who can take command of and direct operations, processes, and all manner of functions in society, intellectuals are, in many ways, matchless or exceptional individuals who are "independent, autonomous, and endowed with a character of their own" (ibid: 186). Unlike Benda, who saw the "multitudes" as being incapable of deep reflection, or the cultivation of the mind and the soul, Gramsci believes that

> [e]very man, . . . outside his professional activity, carries on some form of intellectual activity, that is, he is a philosopher, a man of taste, he participates in a particular conception of the world, has a conscious line of moral conduct, and therefore contributes to sustaining a conception of the world or to modify it, that is, to bring into being, new modes of thought.
>
> (ibid: 187)

From such a delineation, it seems self-evident that, for Gramsci, every community has its fair share of individuals from all walks of life who embody and exemplify the major characteristics of an intellectual life. Gramsci believes that, at some level, every man or woman is an intellectual because most men and women tend to be keen on being involved in either knowledge production or shaping discourses. To shed more light on the issue, he differentiates between two types of intellectuals, namely "traditional" and "organic" ones. The former are those individuals who carry out routine and mundane functions in their day-to-day lives, such as teaching, whereas the latter are special in that they are critical to the functioning of contemporary society by being the voice of reason and conscience in their societies. In other words, on the one hand, "traditional" intellectuals, such as teachers and clerks (or priests), are invaluable assets in their roles as custodians and propagators of useful knowledge and values for the orderly functioning of society. On the other hand, "organic" intellectuals are those individuals who are, or should be, in the vanguard of change in society. Gramsci's major motif in his analysis is that such individuals may well emerge from the category of traditional intellectuals (such as teachers, priests, or doctors) but

20 *Theorising the concept of an intellectual*

that their role changes as they begin to interrogate hegemonic ideologies and beliefs which are associated with the emergence of the class system. According to Henry Giroux, Gramsci expands the category of traditional intellectuals to comprise people such as

> stockbrokers, teachers, researchers, business people, physicians, and other intellectuals who function as purveyors of culture in the limited technical sense of producing a specialized service within a narrow body of knowledge.
>
> (Giroux 2002: 384)

While the responsibilities of these advocates and champions of culture cannot be gainsaid, they are also expected to undertake the kinds of functions which "organic" intellectuals do. Crucially, for Gramsci, it is the unique functions, as well as other attributes which are linked to erudition, that qualify one for the role of an intellectual.

Remarkably, Gramsci's notion of "unique functions" of intellectuals was captured by French philosopher and intellectual Julien Benda. Writing in *La Trahison Des Clercs*, meaning *The Betrayal of the Intellectuals* (first published in 1930 before it appeared in translation in 1955), Benda decries as utterly reckless and irresponsible the conduct and actions of his contemporary intellectuals (whom he described as *clerks*) precisely for having yielded to and embraced what he termed "political passions" (1955: 31) – tendencies and predispositions which would gradually plunge the whole of Europe into the Second World War. He avers that

> we have to admit that the "clerks" now exercise political passions with all the characteristics of passion – the tendency to action, the thirst for immediate results, the exclusive preoccupation with the desired end, the scorn for argument, the excess, the hatred, the fixed ideas.
>
> (ibid: 32)

As I have indicated in Chapter 5, Benda's bitter reproaches of intellectuals' "political passions" centre on the fact that, prior to the Second World War, many intellectuals had so much subscribed to and overstated the notion of difference or Otherness of race that not only did they renege on their obligation of promoting universal values, but they also virtually became accomplices in the kinds of genocides that were taking place in Europe during the war. As Sara Danielsson has put it,

> The work was written . . . as a warning of what Benda had seen in the 1930s on the horizon for Europe. With great unease he saw the unre-

Theorising the concept of an intellectual 21

lenting flood of nationalism, racism and antisemitism, after the horrors of the World War 1.

(2005: 397)

In other words, Benda was immensely disturbed by the way in which intellectuals had opted for co-option into politics where they found themselves legitimising totalitarian regimes instead of performing their noble task of acting as guardians of knowledge in the form of liberal and eternal values. Danielsson goes further to argue that

> Julien Benda's work stands in judgement of all intellectuals who were capable of perceiving the emerging dangers in Europe but chose to close, or avert their eyes.

(ibid: 404)

Benda goes further to inveigh against intellectuals by pinpointing a troubling conflict at the core of their work at the time. He states that

> [t]o have as his function the pursuit of eternal things and yet to believe he becomes greater by concerning himself with the State – that is the view of the modern "clerk".

(1955: 32)

Clearly, Benda must have found it utterly incongruous to see intellectuals holding to political passions when their role in society was to aspire to and live for the ideals of social justice. Thus, Europe learned the hard way, particularly after the two world wars, with dangerous levels of anti-Semitism leading to the Holocaust during the Second World War. All this happened because the idea of identity at the time was based on hard views of ethnic and racial supremacy and purity, with intellectuals not ready to call into question such kinds of warped thinking. The Holocaust remains an enduring reminder of the fate and precarious position of minorities in our communities, where they are subjected to all kinds of ills, such as racial abuse, ethnic cleansing, and xenophobic attacks. So many Jews died in concentration camps because, for many Germans, the idea of community, hence identity, was based on hard views of ethnic or racial purity. It is not surprising that, around the same time, such lopsided thinking was taken up in South Africa through the ideology of apartheid – an ideology of racial discrimination whose replication and application would horrify the entire world before it was dismantled in the 1990s.

Taking his cue from both Julien Benda and Antonio Gramsci, Edward Said would elaborate on the two types of intellectuals which Gramsci

22 Theorising the concept of an intellectual

had identified as being germane to the success of every society. Said also introduces, on the one hand, what Gramsci had termed traditional intellectuals – individuals such as "teachers, priests, and administrators, who continue to do the same things from generation to generation" (Said 2003: 379). On the other hand, Said names Gramsci's second category of "organic" intellectuals as people who were "directly connected to classes or enterprises that use intellectuals to organise interests, gain more power, get control" (ibid: 379). Said goes on at great length to expound on both Benda's and Gramsci's notion of an organic intellectual, by stating that

> the intellectual is an individual with a specific public role in society that cannot be reduced simply to being a faceless professional, a competent member of a class just going about her/his business. The central fact . . . is . . . that the intellectual is an individual endowed with a faculty for representing, embodying, articulating a message, a view, an attitude, philosophy, or opinion to, as well as for a public. And this role has an edge to it, and cannot be played without a sense of being someone whose place it is publicly to raise embarrassing questions, to confront orthodoxy, and dogma (rather than to produce them), to become some-one who cannot easily be co-opted by government or corporations, and whose *raison d'être* is to represent all those people and issues that are routinely forgotten and swept under the rug. The intellectual does so on the basis of universal principles: that all human beings are entitled to decent standards of behavior concerning freedom and justice from worldly powers or nations, and that deliberate or inadvertent violations of these standards need to be testified and fought against courageously.
>
> (ibid: 382)[2]

It is clear that Benda's ideas about intellectuals, which were consolidated into the Gramscian vision of "organic" intellectuals, are what Edward Said has expounded on and embraced. After Benda, Said states that an "organic" intellectual is one who exhibits particularly praiseworthy attributes, an act which entails wedding their superior skills and intense, restless intelligence to particular causes, notably freedom – causes which remind us what it means to be human. For example, an intellectual is somebody who asks probing questions about various forms of knowledge and governance, speaks out against orthodoxy or dogma (around ideology), spurns any attempts to be co-opted into government, and demonstrates great regard for universal values of what it means to be human. In other words, what is quite striking here is the fact that Edward Said presents an intellectual as a unique and gifted personality who participates fully in the discourses that merit attention in society and ensures that she or he is at the forefront of framing

Theorising the concept of an intellectual 23

public opinion. Such an individual has a definite mission of bringing about change in society.

Like Antonio Gramsci and Edward Said before him, Michel Foucault has furthered or expanded the discourse on intellectuals, seeing them in terms of specific functions they are linked with in society. Thus, he states that

> what must . . . be taken into account in the intellectual is not "the bearer of universal values". Rather, it's the person occupying a specific position – but whose specificity is linked, in a society like ours, to the general functioning of an apparatus of truth. In other words, the intellectual has three-fold specificity: that of his class position (whether as petty bourgeois in the service of capitalism or "organic" intellectual of the proletariat); that of his condition of life and work, linked to his condition as an intellectual (his field of research, his place in a laboratory, the political and economic demands to which he submits or against which he rebels, in the university, the hospital etc); lastly, the specificity of the politics of truth in our societies. And it's with this last factor that his position can take on general significance.
>
> (2001: 317–318)

Thus, for Foucault, an intellectual is defined in terms of three specific attributes which she or he must embody as a mandate to carry out three distinctive functions in society. The first specific task involves serving the various classes of society. The second task relates to the academic or ivory tower intellectual, who happens to be a subject specialist in a university and plays the role of advancing knowledge in that field or area of specialty. The last attribute, and one with a telling impact on society, involves the intellectual's involvement in political discourses for purposes of democracy and the enrichment of political life. Whether one is a member of the bourgeoisie, a university lecturer, or a politician, an intellectual is an embodiment of "universal values", meaning particular truths and values which teach us what it means to be human. For Foucault, it is the "politics of truth" which should be the defining quality of an intellectual. In short, critical thinking is fundamental to being a successful intellectual. For example, as a philosopher and serious critical thinker, Foucault is remembered for having come up with the link between notions of discourse and truth. He arrived at the conclusion that the nexus between power and knowledge makes several disciplines of knowledge produce individuals who are interested in power.

Penultimately, Julia Kristeva has made an intriguing and appealing contribution to the debate on intellectuals through her use of the expression "dissident intellectuals". Motivated by a deep conviction that intellectuals

24   *Theorising the concept of an intellectual*

should be socially and politically engaged, Kristeva identifies three types of what she calls *intellectual dissidents*, namely,

> [f]irst, . . . the rebel who attacks political power. He transforms the dialectic of law-and-desire into a war waged between *Power* and *Resentment*. Secondly, there is the psychoanalyst, who transforms the dialectic of law-and-desire into a contest between *death* and *discourse*. Thirdly, there is the writer who experiments with the limits of identity, producing texts where the law does not exist outside language.
>
> (1986: 295)

Kristeva sees an intellectual as a radical or revolutionary figure who embodies and shows deep resentment towards the status quo and struggles to campaign for or bring about change through various ways, activities, or missions, which include activism (in politics) or writing fiction (in literature). For Kristeva, such a "dissident" intellectual is a reformist through and through.

Finally, Noam Chomsky asserts that society needs "value-oriented intellectuals so that democracy can survive" (1978: 14). For Chomsky, a nation-state as we know it is rife with injustices, notably the lack of democracy, and so it is the role of intellectuals to condemn all forms of injustice in a nation.

Who is an African intellectual?

Considering that the idea of an intellectual is located in a broad spectrum of ideas, although political convention suggests that the notion African identity is linked with the idea of blackness, or the black race, the hard reality is that the African continent is not so bounded an entity as to make its identity confined to the idea of only the black race. This is because, for centuries, Africa has been home to people of various races, and so African, or Africanist, intellectuals could be any individuals, notably black, white, Indian, and Arab denizens of Africa, who have been shaped by the African experience. As Anthony Appiah has put it, there are "numerous examples from multiple domains of what . . . being African means" (1992: 177). Here, Appiah points to the fact that the idea of an African is not limited to the black race, as there are other realms of defining who an African is. Further, in defining an African intellectual, Francis Nesbitt states that

> African intellectuals . . . are characterized by the specificity of their intellectual concerns, such as Pan-Africanism, apartheid, development, and the question of language, rather than race or geography.
>
> (2003: 274)

Theorising the concept of an intellectual   25

Thus, like Appiah, for Nesbitt, an African intellectual need not be defined by the colour of his or her skin. For example, the late Ali Mazrui, who was a Kenyan of Indian descent, was always referred to as an African intellectual. Further, during the era of apartheid in South Africa, there were many white writers of fiction who were typically African, or "Africanist", intellectuals in the way their fiction bore witness to the ravages of colonialism in the form of the apartheid system. In their writing, most of the white writers, or intellectuals, notably Alan Paton, Athol Fugard, and Nadine Gordimer, to cite only three examples, introduced ideas of liberalism and humanism to be at the core of South African identity. Born and bred in Africa, these white libertarian writers of fiction which challenged the apartheid system had unmistakably been shaped by the African experience. Thus, rather than race, it is the unique kind of passion one has for a particular responsibility which defines one as an African intellectual. Nesbitt goes on to state that "intellectuals provide meanings to situations, guidelines for escaping from oppression, as well as visions of alternative conditions" (ibid: 274). In other words, intellectuals are visionaries who are capable of transforming people's lives by acting as a bulwark against all forms of extremism in society.

Yet again, when one thinks of the period of apartheid during which some of the best artists, or writers of fiction, were white people, then it is plausible to argue that the idea of race is extraneous to the notion of an African intellectual since some of the best intellectuals in the realm of writing fiction were white people. Interestingly, apart from black writers of fiction whose work used to question colonialism, a good number of white writers who had been shaped by the African experience would become acclaimed writers, considering that their fiction exposed the perils of apartheid. Thus, real African intellectuals are born thinkers in domains such as nationalism, political activism, fiction, music, and many other spheres of life. This delineation of an African intellectual is interesting considering that most black African politicians paint the notion of African identity with a broad brush, meaning it is based on the reality of the majority black race. But, for scholars such Appiah and Nesbitt, when one looks at the inhabitants of the African continent, it is difficult to draw the line between who is an African and who is a non-African. For these scholars, the idea of nativism does not constitute the main element of African intellectualism, as there are different angles and inflections of the word "Africa". Thus, there is a seismic shift with regard to who an African intellectual is. After all, the term *Africa* is a polysemy, a floating signifier, because when it emerged during colonialism, rather than refer to the entire continent, as well as its majority black people, the word *Africa* referred to the northern part of the African continent, which was part of the Roman Empire. Owing to the subtleties of the word *Africa*, as well as taking into account all the specifications of who an intellectual is, at

26 *Theorising the concept of an intellectual*

both "traditional" and "organic" levels, an African intellectual is the kind of thinker, irrespective of race, who acts as a self-appointed custodian of public morals, as well as the champion of various rights and freedoms. The defining characteristic of such an intellectual is the ability to address the burning problems which the African continent continues to face.

The evolution of African intellectuals

Considering that there are various delineations of who an African intellectual is, the evolution of African intellectuals shows a trajectory which is a varied one. Crucially, the fact that the African continent was at different times subjected to all kinds of subjugation, such as slavery and colonialism, the kind of trajectory of African intellectuals can be fully understood and appreciated on four different levels. Thus, one can talk about pre-colonial intellectuals, colonial or pre-independence intellectuals, post-colonial, post-independence intellectuals, and modern intellectuals.

Firstly, it is quite clear that in pre-colonial Africa, there used to be particular and special kinds of black people who were deserving of the designation intellectuals – the term used broadly to refer to the kinds of individuals who, at the time, were at the core of the production and shaping of local knowledge which defined so-called inherited black African cultures and traditions. Even before white people arrived in Africa (with the kind of knowledge which was based on modernity, for instance, education and Christianity, there were some black people who wielded power in their societies in the form of holding or commanding positions, such as traditional kings (or chiefs), growers, merchandisers, medicine men (and women), sorcerers, soothsayers, and diviners (or seers). What all these groups had in common was the fact that they were traditional intellectuals in the sense that they were at the forefront of traditional knowledge production in order to help people in what were typically traditional societies. Most of such knowledge was based on tradition which had been handed down from earlier generations. As well as making all sorts of prognostications about the future, at the core of such traditional thinkers, or intellectuals, was their capacity to describe, formulate, explain, and interpret traditional reality in its various formulations and understandings, largely according to how it had been handed down from the previous generations.

Secondly, during the era of slavery when many black people had been trafficked to Europe and America, a particular group of black intellectuals emerged to address the issue of race. As opposed to traditional intellectuals, these were a learned type of black intellectuals. For example, W. E. B. Du Bois was one black American who represented a paradigm for black African intellectuals in that, as a pseudo-intellectual, he was a fairly well-educated black man who advocated the idea of social reform and civil rights

Theorising the concept of an intellectual 27

in America. In short, Du Bois called into question the issue of identity which was based on binaries, or the dualities of the racial categories of white and black – the kinds of representations which had led to the acts of slavery and colonialism. Other intellectuals who would follow in the footsteps of Du Bois were scholars such as Frantz Fanon, who, as a prominent post-colonial thinker, came up with the notion of Manicheanism as defining the colonial world at the time. For Fanon, the idea of Manicheanism marked and characterised the colonised world, which was defined in terms of Self and Other so that, while the colonised was portrayed in denigrating terms, the coloniser used to enjoy the psychological pleasures of racial superiority.

Thirdly, during colonialism, there were already large populations of people of white and Indian races in Africa. Thus, it is not surprising that the number of writers of fiction whose work was a discourse against colonialism included both black and white people. While in what used to be Southern Rhodesia (currently Zimbabwe), Doris Lessing was writing about the dangers of colonialism, South Africa had both black and white writers whose role in interrogating colonialism was remarkable. Thus, apart from black writers of fiction, such as Ezekiel Mphahlele and Njabulo Ndebele, South Africa had white writers, such as Alan Paton, Athol Fugard, and Nadine Gordimer, to mention a few examples.

Fourthly, and remarkably, from the years leading up to the end of colonial rule in Africa until well into the second decade of the twenty-first century, Africa produced the kinds of liberal and forward-looking black intellectuals who fit the various schemata as spelt out by scholars such as Antonio Gramsci, Julien Benda, Edward Said, Noam Chomsky, and Julia Kristeva. Those individuals who found themselves having to confront and challenge colonialism have not been perceived as *intellectuals* in the conventional sense of intellectuals who belong to the class of the literati or intelligentsia. But, for Walter Bgoya, all pioneering politicians were intellectuals of a kind. Strikingly, as he has put it,

> [i]n the struggles for independence, the generation of leaders – Kenyatta, Nkrumah, Nyerere, Lumumba, and Senghor among those who did not have to wage armed struggle, and among those who had to, the Mandelas (Nelson and Winnie), Agostinho Neto, Edward Mondlane, Amilcar Cabral, Samora Machel, Mohamed A. Babu in Zanzibar and Robert Mugabe – were intellectuals of this kind. The legacy of the South African Communist Party, exemplified by Chris Hani, Joe Slovo, and Ruth First is of many committed revolutionary intellectuals who contributed enormously to the political education of militants within the ANC with which the CP was allied.
>
> (2014: 111)

28 *Theorising the concept of an intellectual*

For Bgoya, as revolutionaries, these thinkers were intellectuals in the broadest sense of the word as articulated by Antonio Gramsci and expounded on by Edward Said – the sense of an intellectual as that "individual who is endowed with a faculty for representing, embodying, articulating a message, a view, an attitude, a philosophy, or opinion to, as well as for a public" (Said 2003: 382). In other words, rather than allow themselves to be manipulated by all forms of knowledge which are linked to people who wield power, an intellectual is the kind of person who develops a turn of mind which is likely to go against conventional ways of thinking – the kind of thinking which is likely to be superficial and simplistic. This explains why an intellectual's critical independence of mind enables him or her to ask difficult questions which relate to all forms of knowledge. Further, Bgoya goes on to expand the category of intellectuals in Africa to include what he calls "mainstream intellectuals" (2014: 112), meaning scholars or members of the intelligentsia. The last category of progressive intellectuals he identifies is that of "activists in the wider community – militants in labour organisations, sports clubs, artists and musicians" (ibid: 112). But, as will be seen in Chapter 3, after independence, many such intellectuals were either conflicted about their roles or just chose to renege on their obligations of serving the people.

Finally, after the end of colonialism, the African continent would produce the kind of post-colonial, post-independence intellectuals who would either form the primary ruling elites or members of the opposition. Many intellectuals would become either opposition leaders or writers of fiction who were prepared to challenge the ruling elites for the lack of progress in domains such as democracy and development. Such intellectuals also challenged radical nationalism, as well as all forms of marginalisation in society, which had led to all kinds of ethnic tensions, such as wars and genocides. Some intellectuals, especially writers, went on to deal with other problems the African continent has always grappled with, notably the triple ills of ignorance, disease, and hunger, as well as related problems which have to do with the lack of various freedoms in realms such as gender and sexuality.

Chapter summary

There is no doubt that intellectuals are an amorphous but gifted and high-minded class of people from across a broad spectrum of society, notably clerks, political activists, university teachers, journalists, pundits, teachers, social activists from various spheres of society, musicians, and many other categories of enlightened and progressive individuals whose distinguishing feature is a fair-minded approach to knowledge, as well as the way they dispense judgement in society. As theorised by the various scholars in this chapter, what such individuals have in common is their ability to

Theorising the concept of an intellectual 29

participate in commendable virtues through their mediation and shaping of public discourses – something which is of critical significance as far as the issue of transformation is concerned. Such transformation should focus on amelioration in realms such as physical development, education, health, human rights, identity, various freedoms, and several spheres of life. In a word, rather than being sterile or non-creative technocrats, genuine intellectuals are people who are imbued with and have learnt to cultivate the spirit of impartiality and justice as the founding principles or ideals of a stable society. Such impartiality arises from the fact that intellectuals are the kind of individuals who have or develop the kind logic, or thinking, which is about transcending people's various horizons in life, particularly in terms of issues such as cultural, religious, and ideological beliefs or certainties, as well as political affiliations. Thus, through all forms of agency, such as artwork, fiction, and activism, an intellectual is an individual who becomes the voice of reason, the spokesperson for the powerless, a mouthpiece of the weak, and the voice of conscience in society. It is such disinterestedness that makes intellectuals real think-tanks – the mass of some of the most important individuals in society precisely because they have a moral duty to perform in the various work placement services.

Notes

1 Benda's understanding of intellectuals – a group he labelled "clerks" – is unique in that it is both Socratic and even pre-Socratic in its signification. Hence, he views intellectuals as people who are, in many ways, comparable to great philosophers or teachers like Socrates and Jesus Christ. For Benda, intellectuals are such rare and superior beings that they are so innately accomplished they stand for universal values and, for that reason, should lead society.
2 Like Julien Benda and Antoni Gramsci, an intellectual has to stand for justice and truth in society.

2 The "ivory tower" intellectual

It is perfectly plausible to argue that the expression and notion of an *ivory tower* per se is traceable to biblical times. This is because, as used in the Bible by the writer of Song of Songs, the expression "ivory tower" is part of a description of a woman of gorgeous looks and impressive beauty, one whose "neck is like a tower of ivory" (7:4), meaning she looks glamourous. Then, in the book of Genesis, we learn that, as people who spoke different languages, the Babylonians wanted to remain united so as to steer clear of any eventuality of dispersal to other parts of the earth. Thus the people came together, and their leaders said "Come, let us build ourselves a city and a tower with its top in the sky" (11:1–9), or the heavens. This structure would later be called the Tower of Babel, which would link the people of Babylon to their God in heaven. However, the Babylonians did not succeed in their efforts to erect this type of super structure, which was meant to connect them to their creator. But remarkably, as David Demers has put it,

> scientists for the past two centuries or so have been building a tower of sorts, only this time the attempt is to build one composed of knowledge rather than bricks . . . scientists see their tower of knowledge as a means for solving social problems – such as poverty, crime, drug abuse, inequality, discrimination, unemployment, abuse of power – that alienate people and groups from modern society.
>
> (2011: 10)[1]

For Demers, scientists came up with the tower or structure of knowledge as a surrogate for the Tower of Babel. Thus the tower of knowledge became a means of finding resolutions to society's problems. Gradually, the expression "ivory tower" came to refer to a sanctum, or something of a retreat, for the educated in society who, feeling gifted and privileged, avoided all the problems which are associated with normal life.

The *"ivory tower"* intellectual   31

What one finds interesting about the phrase "ivory tower" is the fact that the expression whose initial meaning (of linking the people of Babylon to God), which used to be a positive one in every sense, would later begin to resonate with somewhat negative connotations simply because of its reference to universities, as well as related institutions of higher learning – special locations which house the educated class of society. These are institutions which are seen as sanctums which harbour a particular class of people who are designated as intellectuals, also variously known as academics, whose apparent detachment from the practical problems and difficulties of ordinary existence makes them look at life with some kind of Olympian indifference. Academics are seen as people who lead sheltered lives in the ivory towers. At least, that is how some ordinary people understand the notion of "ivory tower" intellectuals. Other terms which have the same sense as "ivory tower" are the academy, or academe. Used and understood in a rather standard and conventional way of being linked to the notion of "ivory tower", the word *intellectual* tends to be more germane and pertinent to a category of people called academics whose task is to teach in a university and who are expected to undertake research in their various disciplines or areas of their speciality.

Thus, as opposed to other groups in society, notably teachers, priests, or doctors, who happen to be leaders in their respective lines of work, it must be said that ivory tower intellectuals, or university teachers, also certainly deserve the designation *intellectuals*. As I argue in this chapter, rather than simply ensconce themselves in the academic sanctum, "ivory tower" intellectuals need to be think-tanks who are prepared to bring about change in society through the application of the various kinds of knowledge which they either produce or promote for the good of society. Since they find themselves in the marketplace of ideas, academics need to play the prophetic role of being objective political commentators who are prepared to question whatever they see as evidently lopsided ways of presenting and articulating political and other ideas. Ivory tower intellectuals must ask probing questions which are meant to unsettle orthodoxies and dogmas which are harmful to society.

The nature of the universities

Sheldon Gardner has made some important observations regarding the nature and function of universities as sanctums or "ivory towers" of knowledge production. In an attempt to give credence to the notion of the *ivory tower*, he claims that "when universities were first established during the Middle Ages, they were intended to be insulated institutions" (1992: 239).

32 The "ivory tower" intellectual

In other words, they were sheltered institutions for the meritocracy who would later be known as mainstream intellectuals. Gardner's assertion is at the core of the tag *ivory tower*, which is associated with universities as educational establishments where pundits are completely cut off from the day-to-day reality which ordinary citizens experience in society. Gardner confirms this state of affairs when he asserts that universities were "a community of intellectuals to further research and to accumulate knowledge without the interference of the Church or state" (ibid: 240) and that "[t]he scholars who gathered in these towers were supposed to educate or train" (ibid: 240). In other words, the expectation of an ivory tower (as an institution) is that it should harbour individuals who are highly educated and trained in various fields of their speciality. Further, Gardner makes a point of emphasising the centrality of the universities in furthering knowledge by stating that

> most universities were producing educated priests and monks (an education heavy on dogma, theology, and philosophy, and one in which contemplation and reflection on traditional wisdom were so highly valued) that many academicians maintain that esoteric, other-worldly mindset that is associated with the term ivory tower today.
>
> (ibid: 240)

It is difficult to quibble with what Gardner states in the preceding quotation because with its polymorphous ensemble of intellectuals who are expected to understand the nature of philosophy or knowledge in general, the university still remains an embodiment of a sheltered environment which abounds with a good number of individuals most of whom are of high erudition and exemplary scholarship. In other words, most universities have intellectuals who are representative of individuals who need to perform the function of being the consciousness, as well as the conscience, of society in that they are regarded as bearers of particular eternal and universal truths, or values, which they attain through learning and knowledge production. Variously called university teachers, academics (or academicians), men or women of letters, and scholars, the kinds of intellectuals who are associated with the *ivory tower* are often regarded as relatively privileged individuals simply because they are located in "the safe and specialised confines of the university" (Giroux 2002: 385) and their task is to build "towers" of knowledge or carry out works of scholarship, as well as teaching. In various universities or institutions of higher learning globally, these individuals are expected to demonstrate scientific and systematic expertise in their respective fields or spheres of interest and speciality. Thus, conventionally, the presumption is that these types of intellectuals have specialised knowledge and their

The "ivory tower" intellectual 33

placement in the *ivory tower* makes them assets whose knowledge is meant to benefit society. Remarkably, given that some critics see the university as a sphere which should remain "a depoliticized site and limit pedagogy to the arid imperatives of discipline-bound professionalization and specialization" (ibid: 386) and believe that the "so-called radical academic" "is interested mainly in career advancement and cushy rewards of tenure rather than acting as a proponent of social change"(ibid: 385, echoing Russell Jacoby 1987), it has been argued that such intellectuals are nothing but "sterile technocrats" (Giroux 2002: 385). In short, it is assumed that intellectuals are seen as non-creative and unproductive experts. Granted, there will always be people who thrive on all forms of opportunism and hence remain idle and unproductive in institutions where they are expected to do their best. From the preceding remarks, it is such a pity that some critics should portray the university – universally the hub of knowledge production – in such a negative light. Of course, this is not surprising. Indeed, this is because universities also harbour certain individuals who are there just to earn a living. However, it is important that intellectuals in the ivory tower be cognisant of the fact that any attempt to display such insouciant indifference to the role they are supposed to play disadvantages society. As individuals who are expected to be dealing with the kind of knowledge which is the avant-garde, ivory tower intellectuals should also be in the vanguard of change in society by helping it to develop and transform in various spheres of life.

African "ivory tower" intellectuals since the end of colonialism

With the "ivory tower" tag which has such rebarbative overtones, how do ivory tower intellectuals shed such a negative association with their calling and become typically "organic" intellectuals in the Saidian sense so they can benefit society? How best can an important public sphere such a university produce "organic" intellectuals? Working in various fields, such as the natural sciences, social sciences, and the humanities, how do these intellectuals justify their existence in the academe? Walter Bgoya echoes Mical Cabral in his argument which says that it is this category of intellectuals which "has to work out strategies to enable it to continue work for the interests of the people despite and also because of the barriers in the way" (2014: 113). It is vitally important to address these questions because it would be amiss if knowledge production in the ivory tower were just about feeding the egos of all types of academics, including professors. Of course, academics or scholars have ideas and do undertake various forms of research which should have the impact of "solving social problems and impacting public policy" (Demers 2011: 14). However, apart from

34 *The "ivory tower" intellectual*

teaching, the mission of the university remains knowledge production and its impact on society. Researchers should have definite meaning to society in the sense of making sure that citizens benefit from the kind of research or knowledge they produce. In other words, knowledge produced in the ivory tower institutions should be used to "fix social problems or to better understand human behavior" (ibid: 28). Put another way, ivory tower intellectuals should make sure that their knowledge is used to transform society. This entails that, in their various areas of speciality, ivory tower intellectuals should ensure that they make immense contributions to the success of the education system by developing their disciplines in such a way as to adapt and make them accessible at various levels of schooling, as well as for the wider public.

For Henry Giroux, "ivory tower" intellectuals should engage in the kind of discourse which

> contains the promise of producing a revitalised language about public life and intellectual leadership. More specifically, such a discourse offers the potential for raising on a national level serious questions regarding the relevance of the university as a critical public sphere, the political significance of cultural work taking hold across an emerging number of public spheres and pedagogical sites, and the necessity of reclaiming the language of the public as part of a broader discourse for revitalizing the discourses of democracy and social justice.
>
> (2002: 384)

What Giroux is trying to put across is the fact that intellectuals must be prepared to carry out the kind of research that is strategic in that, ultimately, it should help society to ameliorate all kinds of problems, including those to do with democracy, human rights, and other related freedoms. The university should be the location for the origin of public discourse. Thus, the kind of research which intellectuals carry out must enable them to embrace the kind of language which should fully address issues of social justice in society. For example, natural scientists can help the general public to appreciate the physical world and use their quantitative research methods to generate knowledge that directly addresses problems in society. Similarly, the kind of research carried out by intellectuals in the domain of the humanities (which includes social sciences and the arts) can also feed into the lives of ordinary people in society in a direct way because the humanities deal with notions of what it means to be human. Thus disciplines such as the arts and the humanities should play a role of acting as useful interventions in the humanities and, by extension, in society.

How can African "ivory tower" intellectuals play a prophetic role in Africa?

Since the end of colonialism, Africa has produced a great number of "ivory tower" intellectuals, individuals who are "often of modest origin but endowed with high level of education" (Charle 2015: 41). As a professional group who are just a fraction of the population, this category of intellectuals see themselves as being radically different from other great thinkers whom society produces, notably fiction writers and musicians. Since the end of colonialism, Africa, like other parts of the Western world, has turned out countless *ivory tower* intellectuals who should have been pivotal to the development of their societies. As "islands of intellectual activity" (Gardner 1992), it would seem that universities do not matter today as they did in the Middle Ages when monks were the kind of intellectuals who would teach the people the religious ideology or world view of the time. Therefore, the impact of *ivory tower* intellectuals in Africa must be seen in the areas of visibility or the ability to make themselves available to and educate the public. Further, intellectuals of this nature must undertake the kind of research which is strategic or applicable in the sense of helping society. Given that universities "were and are expected to meet practical goals and were and are influenced by the changing needs and interests of society" (Gardner 1992: 240), *ivory tower* intellectuals in Africa cannot afford to be oblivious to or ignorant of what happens in the wider society where politics seems central to people's lives. For that reason, labels such as "the ideology of professionalization, or the cult of expertise" (Giroux 2002: 392) – labels which are associated with *ivory tower* intellectuals – should be dispensed with so as to enable these intellectuals to maximise their skills by combining scholarship with public service in ways which enrich and deepen the goals of democracy and social justice. It is worth reflecting on "the role that public intellectuals might play within and outside of the academy in linking critical knowledge with the political and social realities of people's everyday lives" (ibid: 397). Granted, it is expected that an *ivory tower* intellectual demonstrates attributes such as a sharp focus or an academic poise or disposition in that she or he is sceptical of knowledge claims, as well as demonstrating authority and being immersed in cutting edge research which benefits society. Further, as society's cultural capital, to use Pierre Bourdieu's expression, intellectuals should not demonstrate callous indifference or take knowledge production as the only preoccupation that should feed their egos. But, crucially, they need to increase their visibility through the public media, such as newspapers, and iconographic media, such as the television, where they should be seen to be dealing with issues which impact public policy, as well as

36   *The "ivory tower" intellectual*

the wider public. Thus, through their research, ivory tower intellectuals in Africa should be involved in providing unremitting commentary on their work's relevance to society. They should demonstrate and open new dimensions of looking at various aspects of knowledge. Further, particularly in the arts and the humanities, ivory tower intellectuals could become innovative by introducing the language of political correctness so as to help society embrace such language, particularly in the categories of race, gender, sexuality, class, and other classifications. This is because any failure to use such language has often caused all sorts of problems on the African continent, including gender violence, ethnic wars, genocide, and xenophobic attacks.

As I show in Chapter 5, rather than simply revel in the standard practice of teaching in a university, as well as participating in knowledge production, let ivory tower intellectuals in Africa stand for the ideas and values of change or transformation. Thus, instead of using the ivory tower as the only anchor for their lives, they should also explore and use other outlets or avenues to demonstrate the value of the knowledge they have internalised or mastered. For example, African "ivory tower" intellectuals could become producers of radio and television talk shows and documentaries, where each intellectual gives a critical commentary on contemporary issues in domains of knowledge, such as politics, economics, culture, and other spheres of know-how or expertise. Such intellectuals could also become useful critics in national newspapers, where they could be engaged in debates about prevailing issues. Crucially, "ivory tower" intellectuals ought to become invaluable intervention in public discourses by ensuring that they pitch their work at the kind of levels which will be accessible to and understood and appreciated by a general audience or the broader public so that people are well-informed about various issues which matter in society. Such intervention by "ivory tower" intellectuals could mean that issues such as democracy and other kinds of freedoms will be taken seriously in their societies.

Chapter summary

Conventionally understood as authentic intellectuals primarily because of their link and involvement with knowledge production in academia, "ivory tower" intellectuals are men and women who possess the kind of expertise which enables them to teach in universities and other institutions of higher learning, where they are also expected to undertake research. Thus, because of their specialised knowledge, African intellectuals of ivory tower bent should act as role models by making great efforts to remain visible and available for crucial interventions in society by contextualising some relevant knowledge in such a way they are able to shed light on what happens on the ground. Ivory tower intellectuals should play the prophetic role by

The *"ivory tower" intellectual* 37

making use of their unique positions in academia to come up with useful and well-thought-out prognoses for what the future holds for the people. In particular, African "ivory tower" intellectuals are the type of individuals who should minister to and make a contribution towards a fulfilling life for the people by being at the forefront of helping civil society to cultivate the kind of critical consciousness which paves the way for the kind of change, or transformation, which points to a civilised and cultured way of life on the African continent. Not only should such intellectuals be avant-garde thinkers in terms of helping politicians to find solutions to all kinds of problems, but they should also be available to demonstrate the link between what are evidently metaphysical and esoteric forms of knowledge and ideas and hard, social reality.

Note

1 For Demers, the notion of the ivory tower is now a metaphor for universities (i.e., places of knowledge production).

3 The dilemmas of African intellectuals since the end of colonialism

How modern African intellectuals should steer clear of such sticking points

The kinds of dilemmas which African intellectuals have faced since the end of colonialism are so worrying and disturbing that, in the last fifty years or so, there has been very little progress on the continent, as intellectuals of various shades are hardly given the opportunity to make contribution to society's progress. Generally, the predicaments I pinpoint are commonplace in the post-colonial world, including Asia and Latin American countries. However, the dilemmas which I spell out in this chapter relate to the largely hostile political climate which scholars have pinpointed and highlighted as being the stumbling block to carrying out meaningful intellectual activities on the African continent. The political climate in Africa is so damaging because politicians control the societies in an overbearing manner. Such uncongenial and repulsive conditions which emerged following the end of colonial rule point to the kind of predicaments which mostly black African intellectuals have gone through on the African continent. In other words, there has been alienation of African intellectuals in many African states, particularly tyrannical ones. It is factors such as self-seeking black African politicians and uncritical adherence to notions such as nationalism and Pan-Africanism which have largely hobbled intellectual work on the continent, thereby forcing intellectuals to either leave the continent or yield to co-option by the ruling elites. As to why many intellectuals leave Africa, Francis Nesbitt has argued that

> African politicians are partly to blame for the exodus because of the political and economic crises they create and the lack of recognition of the contributions of African intellectuals.
>
> (2008: 19)

Interestingly, Africa has always had intellectuals of various shades and stripes who would interrogate the discourse of colonialism while cast in different moulds, such as nationalists, "ivory tower" intellectuals, or

The dilemmas of African intellectuals 39

simply "dissident" intellectuals, to use Julia Kristeva's expression. In addition to this category of intellectuals, there have always been those intellectuals across the continent who "have contributed to the shaping of Pan-Africanism" (Mkandawire 2005a: 8). As I indicated in Chapter 1, by and large, most African independence movements were led by individuals of great imagination and clearly of intellectual bent. In fact, it is this first category of individuals, or intellectuals, who would make a lasting impression on the future generations and hence have come to be known by the endearing expression "pioneering politicians", precisely because of the contribution they "made to the total liberation of the entire continent from colonialism to apartheid" (Bgoya 2014: 114). For instance, the African National Congress of South Africa – a party which fought against the apartheid regime – is a case in point of a party "where intellectuals played a central role in the struggle" (ibid: 4). It is interesting to note that nationalists are regarded as intellectuals precisely because they were questioning the nature and logic of the colonial rule or government. These unique individuals were intellectuals in their own right in that they played a vitally important role not only in conscientising their populace about the horrors of colonialism per se but also by either negotiating a settlement or just standing up against colonial oppression by taking up arms against the apartheid government.

As I made clear in Chapter 1, most avant-garde political activists who were at the forefront of the anti-colonial struggle were themselves intellectuals who were either missionary- or Western-educated individuals. This means that they were intellectuals in the sense that they had been involved in questioning and challenging Western practices of colonialism which had left the black people a stereotyped and subjugated racial group. However, it is a matter of tragic irony that, once in power, some of these mostly black African intellectuals, turned politicians, were "not interested in advancing the interests of the poor and the marginalized masses" (Bogya 2014: 113). In fact, for a good number of them, power became their undoing, for "the more they stayed in power, the more entrenched they became in living the good life, taking it as their right and embarking on private wealth accumulation . . . and corruption facilitated by agents of foreign and local corporate interests" (ibid: 113). Some of these "political" intellectuals could not brook any criticism from other intellectuals who dared to point out that the nationalist projects were going awry owing to factors such as the lack of political vision by politicians, corruption, dictatorial tendencies, political brinkmanship, and other related forms of negativity with regard to governance. Remarkably, if other intellectuals of various bents challenged such trends, they were either penalised or hounded into exile. As Francis Nesbitt has argued, many African intellectuals

40 *The dilemmas of African intellectuals*

are pushed out of their countries after political disturbances at university campuses. Others are exiled because their political perspectives do not correspond to the dominant ideological dispensation of the time. Yet, these same forces that kept them from achieving their full potential at home demonise them for leaving instead of contributing to national development. These tensions between intellectuals and politicians have boiled over frequently in the postcolonial world.

(2008: 19)

Thus, the most disturbing predicament which most liberal and open-minded intellectuals have faced on the African continent is that of being hounded out of their countries simply for providing constructive criticism. Some of these intellectuals were either killed or simply silenced by being co-opted into political leadership. Most of those who were hounded into exile represented post-colonial intellectuals whose hopes of enjoying the fruits of independence were left stillborn most of their lives. In some African countries, this state of affairs has been going on well into the second decade of the twenty-first century.

It might sound tendentious, ironic even, that one should broach and examine the kinds of dilemmas or predicaments black African intellectuals have grappled to overcome since the 1950s as if this is unique to the African continent. However, as I make clear in Chapter 5, European intellectuals practically ran into similar difficulties particularly in the first part of the twentieth century. What is clear is that, after the end of colonialism, mostly black African intellectuals, largely disguised as nationalists, slipped into the role of cheerleading for nationalism after being catapulted into power as political leaders. In the meantime, other intellectuals started cheerleading for those "political" intellectuals who had attained power. In other words, while intellectuals of nationalist bent were cheerleading for ideas such as nationalism and Pan-Africanism, some other intellectuals were looking for opportunities of co-option into tyrannical governments. This state of affairs left intellectuals of liberal inclination no choice but to prepare for self-imposed exile.

The dilemmas of African intellectuals have been further highlighted by Thandika Mkandawire, who has argued that

[t]the nationalist modernity project is inherently fraught with dilemmas that require careful and constant attention. The critical intellectual task is not simply [to] state this rather banal fact but to engage society in acknowledging and addressing . . . such dilemmas. The dilemmas include those of individual and or local rights and national sovereignty; the conflict between the particularism of nationalism and the universal-

The dilemmas of African intellectuals 41

ism of its aspirations; the thin line between unity and uniformity; and cultural homogeneity and provincialism; the trade-off in the development process.

(2005a: 46)

Strikingly, what Mkandawire avers in the preceding quotation is the fact that, from the end of decolonisation to the present, those African intellectuals who wanted to make a positive contribution to society have been adversely affected by serious political malaise owing to a great number of dilemmas which Mkandawire pinpoints, namely "political" intellectuals opting for insular notions, such as cultural uniformity of the entire continent. For example, there is a lack of individual rights in most African countries because of dictatorial tendencies. Further, in the name of nationalism or sovereignty, some groups of people have displayed dangerous forms of provincialism, the kind of insularity which has led to genocides and related forms of black-on-black violence. Crucially, the three chronic ills of illiteracy, hunger, and disease still remain the bane of existence for mostly black Africans largely owing to political brinkmanship or poor governance and an adherence to particular forms of provincialism which are based on nationalism, ethnicity, and religion, to mention a few examples. It is high time that twenty-first-century African intellectuals woke up to the realities of the new age so they can tackle head-on and address such post-colonial dilemmas which have stood in the way of freedom and democracy from the end of colonial rule in Africa well over fifty years ago to the present.

African intellectuals become cheerleaders

As pointed out above, a great number of progressive intellectuals found themselves in a predicament of cheerleading for politicians largely because of the behaviour of the new governing elites. As far as such predicaments of black African intellectuals is concerned, Thandika Mkandawire has observed that, following independence from colonial rule, "[t]he African state has posed a serious dilemma for African intellectuals, at once seductive and menacing" (2005a: 3). In other words, an intellectual who wanted to "speak the truth to power", to use Edward Said's famous expression, would either be co-opted into power or simply marginalised, with the result that a good number of them yielded to co-option and started cheerleading for those political "intellectuals" in power. This observation has corroborating evidence from Walter Bgoya in what he has described as "African governments, and their persecution and marginalisation of the intelligentsia" (2014: 114), with the result that such intellectuals would "endure alienation from their countries of origin" (Nesbitt 2003: 19) and become the

42 *The dilemmas of African intellectuals*

comprador intelligentsia. Members of the comprador class use their national origins, colour and education to serve as spokesmen and intellectual henchmen for organizations such as the World Bank and International Monetary Fund.

(ibid: 25)

Thus, once colonialism was over, those "political" intellectuals who wielded power were not interested in listening to the intelligentsia, with the result that the latter left their countries for international jobs. At the same time, the ruling elites were not keen on advancing the interests of all members of the society, particularly the poor. In short, most "political" intellectuals would not tolerate other clearly progressive intellectuals who would take them to task. Thus, regarding the dictatorial nature of the leaders who took over from colonialists, the kinds of difficulties, or predicaments, which African intellectuals were made to confront in the post-independence era primarily related to the prevailing hostile political climate of the day. Owing to factors such as an uncritical devotion to nationalism, Pan-Africanism, or just the exercise of political brinkmanship by some political leaders, the adverse "post-colonial", political environment did not allow black African intellectuals – be it the intelligentsia or social and political activists – any room to apply their minds to finding solutions to some of the most pressing problems societies faced at the time. Without doubt, there was a growing realisation by progressive intellectuals that those political leaders who had demonstrated their exceptional intellectual abilities during the fight against colonial rule were now either harping on the theme of nationalism and development or simply trying to consolidate power into their hands, thereby not being open to constructive criticism. Thandika Mkandawire further points out some of the dilemmas of the intellectuals, as follows:

[n]ationalism was fraught with many contradictions that severely taxed intellectuals who sought to understand or resolve them. On the one hand, it had adopted the liberal language of "one man, one vote" and the individual right to morally discredit colonialism. On the other hand, its major objective was collective self determination. There was no logical or political reason why, upon the attainment of the latter, the nationalist should respect individual freedom.

(2005a: 16)

The reality implicit in Mkandawire's assertion above is that various freedoms were sacrificed in the name of power, nationalism, and patriotism. Such forms of retrogressive thinking must have been such a sticking point in the lives of intellectuals who had been keen on making a positive and

The dilemmas of African intellectuals 43

valuable contribution towards transforming societies in the new post-colonial nation-states.

Again, as Mkandawire has further put it,

> one of the promises to which the nationalists gave short shrift was democracy. No sooner had they come to power than they found reason to discard the liberal democratic institutions that they had fought for and which had eventually brought them to power. The argument given included the need for strong government and unity, for both "nation-building" and development, and the cultural inappropriateness of Western institutions to African conditions.
>
> (ibid: 16)

In other words, intellectuals of the nationalist bent saw power as a restitution for the fight against colonialism, this at the expense of democracy. It is weird seeing that nationalists, or pioneering politicians, who were former intellectuals themselves, could be so ambivalent about democracy they could not listen to or brook any remedial criticism from progressive intellectuals. No wonder progressive and libertarian intellectuals could hardly understand the notion of nationalism in such a muddled and muddling form.

Further, with the end of colonialism, African intellectuals have been subjected to all manner of dilemmas, including the muddle created by the nexus between intellectual work and Pan-Africanism or nationalism, opportunism, and marginalisation from the political elites. In other words, since the end of colonial rule, nurturing intellectuals who would demonstrate their autonomy and independence of thought has been quite a challenge – the kind of challenge which Thandika Mkandawire pinpoints, as follows:

> [f]rom the earliest days of independence African intellectuals have clamoured for autonomous spaces for their thinking. And not many such spaces were offered by the various oppressive regimes that have reigned in much of Africa since independence.
>
> (2005a: 9)

In other words, most intellectuals, particularly those belonging to the "ivory tower" category of thinkers decided to be part of autonomous spaces for their thinking. Put another way, they decided to remain in the sanctum of the ivory tower, showing no interest in helping society. As far as progressive "ivory tower" intellectuals are concerned, owing to a hostile and adverse political climate which has persisted on the continent for years, a good number of such intellectuals opted to remain what Francis Nesbitt calls the "the comprador intelligentsia" (2003: 25), meaning a class of mostly educated

44 *The dilemmas of African intellectuals*

Africans most of whom decided to leave the continent for the West where they would either teach in Western universities or work as consultants for international organisations, such the IMF or the World Bank. Such scholars are called syncretic intellectuals, meaning those who the moment "they move to the West . . . they face a new environment that forces them to rethink their identities as Africans" (ibid: 21), with the result that, rather than be linked to Africa, they tend to embrace hybrid identities. Little wonder, it is commonly thought in some scholarly circles that, going back to the end of colonial rule, the role of a black African intellectual has remained undefined and indistinct, precisely because most intellectuals realised that their role of acting as champions of conscience in society was always at odds with the expectations of the ruling elites, for whom the notion of nationalism was central to the survival of the new nation-state. As Thandika Mkandawire has so eloquently put it,

> [t]he relationship between nationalism and intellectuals or the intelligentsia has been widely debated. More specifically, there has been interest in explaining the fascination of intellectuals with or their adhesion to nationalism. Some have attributed self-interest by intellectuals whose path to material or professional ascendancy was blocked by the colonizer. National liberation is thus seen as a way of acceding to positions of power. Other less cynical interpretations attribute it to the skills of intellectuals in articulating in coherent form the aspirations of their countrymen and women. Still others attribute to the intellectuals a fascination with a fad – nationalism being one of the products of modernization.
>
> (2005b: 10)

For Mkandawire, some intellectuals' endeavours were encumbered by factors such as an uncritical adherence to nationalism, as well as opportunism, and a lack of definitive intellectual skills which are necessary for change in society. That is why, after most African countries had attained independence, all that most intellectuals of various shades were interested in was power.

Since the end of colonialism, the category of intellectuals who, in common parlance, are known as scholars or academics would hardly make a difference in society. One would have thought that this class of intellectuals' involvement in the nationalist struggles was a blessing in terms of building a vibrant post-colonial African state with people who would help to bring about democratic dispensations across the African continent. This was a time when Africa needed intellectuals who would speak to their countrymen or women, without fear or excess of caution. But the relationship between

The dilemmas of African intellectuals 45

the new political elites and intellectuals would become so fraught that the role of the latter remained on the periphery in the new nation-states. For a long time, any intellectuals found themselves in a predicament with regard to the role they were expected to play in society. This is because, with a few exceptions, black African leaders demonstrate a sense of imperious entitlement to power, thereby leaving the continent mired in confusion. As Sara Marzagora has argued,

> like nativism, nationalism was very strong in post-independence African universities, and many writers, historians, and critics rallied around political leaders and programmes.
>
> (2016: 164)

In other words, the idea of nationalism was seen as being so central to the notion of identity that ivory tower intellectuals were not given any opportunities to become independent thinkers. Instead, while, on the one hand, this state of affairs allowed reactionary intellectuals to easily collaborate with and cheerlead for politicians, on the other hand, liberal and progressive intellectuals' hopes of effecting change in society were utterly dashed. Marzagora goes on to state that such

> growing disillusionment with nationalism . . . in many intellectuals' eyes had been often manipulated to represent narrow, often ethnic, interests and, as such, had proven to be more divisive than cohesive.
>
> (ibid: 165)

Thus politicians' polarising approach to governance meant that intellectuals were stripped of all the power to carry out their business of bringing about change in society. As Mkandawire further contends, "[t]he capacity of the intellectuals to speak truth to power, and their penchant for puncturing myths which were prized in the struggle for independence, were now perceived as divisive and thus inimical to the new nation-state" (2005b: 3). Thus, the intellectuals found themselves at the crossroads of nationalism and Pan-Africanism, on the one hand, and the imperative of belonging to civil society, on the other. As a result, many intellectuals were so marginalised that, in many African countries, they chose to become significant cogs in the political machinery. Such intellectuals who lost their moral stature and obligation by accepting co-option would, in some cases, aid and abet all forms of abuses in the post-colonial state, including ethnic cleansing and genocides. In contrast, those intellectuals who were conscientious and became critical of the ruling elites ended up becoming migrant intellectuals, often because they were hounded into

46 *The dilemmas of African intellectuals*

exile as "victims of government repression" (Nesbitt 2003: 19).[1] In other words, the last dilemma which black African intellectuals have faced has largely been to do with their own spirit of opportunism. There were particular intellectuals who were prepared to sacrifice their intellectual expertise for the material comforts that the new independent nation-states offered. Such intellectuals were prepared to become cheerleaders for ideals, such as patriotism, as well as the political leadership. The idea of intellectuals playing the role of cheerleader for politicians is a euphemistic reference to a particularly disconcerting disposition displayed by those intellectuals who saw fit to start providing support for either political leadership or ideals such as nationalism or Pan-Africanism. In Africa, there are several instances of intellectuals who were seen to cheerlead for political leadership, as well as patriotism. For example, the years between 1980 and the second decade of the twenty-first century saw Zimbabwe have such intellectuals. In these years, we have been a witness to the political situation in Zimbabwe in which some politicised intellectuals left academia in order to serve the Zimbabwean political elites. Once such ivory tower intellectuals succumbed to the tempting and seductive overtures of political life by joining the ruling Zanu PF party, they practically became servants of political aims and passions in that they were prepared to defend the immoral politics of President Robert Mugabe by making sure that no matter how constructive the voice of the opposition was, it was not given an opportunity to flourish. For reasons of pure political opportunism, such individuals used their stature as intellectuals located in academia to legitimise a regime that had lost its moral authority until the country's economy shifted from being the breadbasket of Africa to a basket case. This picture replicated itself at a macro level in the African continent.

At another level, it might be argued that other manifestations of opportunism have been displayed by "comprador" intellectuals who

> can be recognized by their uncritical adoption of the free market ideology of globalization as the solution to Africa's development crisis. They can be seen touring the continent on generously funded research junkets and attending conferences where they defend the global and heap blame upon African countries for corruption, tribalism and ineptitude.
>
> (Nesbitt 2003: 25)

These intellectuals were prompted to leave the African continent for the West because the conditions were not conducive to work in an African country or university. To the extent that they were not prepared to serve their nations, these intellectuals were yielding to some form of opportunism by going to work in societies where they would be fully rewarded for their

The dilemmas of African intellectuals   47

skills. But, at the same time, it is sensible to argue that they were pragmatists in the sense that, as Mkandawire has put it,

> the first wave of the African intelligentsia was absorbed by the state and parastatal bureaucracies. Once indigenization had been achieved, most governments had little motivation for the African university.
>
> (2005b: 23)

In other words, most African politicians have not made African universities appealing enough by providing an inviting atmosphere for doing research, as most governments were not prepared to fund such institutions. This explains why a good number of members of the intelligentsia are prepared to leave African universities for government or parastatals so they can earn more money than is offered at institutions of higher learning.

How can contemporary African intellectuals reclaim the critical roles in Africa's political milieu today?

Africa is a continent of great difficulty, uncertainty, and precariousness. The reality about the African continent is that, apart from a few countries which are progressive bastions as far as the issue of democracy is concerned, most African countries are like laboratories for political change, as the issue of liberal democracy is always under strain. For example, politicians chip away at the idea of democracy by stealing elections. Apart from men of vison, such as the late Nelson Mandela (of South Africa) and Seretse Khama (of Botswana), most politicians suffer from the kind of egomania which makes them think of political power as their entitlement. Most politicians are impervious to any kind of criticism. Given such a hostile and inhibitive nature of politics in Africa – the kind of politics which engenders unspeakable and uncongenial political climates in most African countries – this kind of atmosphere is hardly conducive to the role of progressive intellectuals – individuals who, in their respective domains of knowledge, ought to demonstrate the spirit of initiative, enterprise, and dynamism in order to arrest the negative political climate which is pervasive in most African countries. Thus, firstly, as "political" intellectuals, opposition leaders in manifestly non-democratic countries should be prepared to openly challenge largely blinkered and increasingly dictatorial African leadership which sees the idea of democracy as an intrusion to the idea of governance. Secondly, as for journalists, who are also intellectuals of a kind, rather than whip up any sympathies for politicians, they should openly and unmistakably demonstrate the extent to which politicians' rhetoric is laced with all kinds of leanings, including populism (which entails clinging to power),

48 *The dilemmas of African intellectuals*

ethnicity, and nationalism. Thirdly, through poignant messages in the songs they write and sing, musicians should expose politicians' ego-trips, which should be halted. Fourthly, government mandarins, or functionaries whose tasks predispose them to the roles of intellectuals, should employ either open-mindedness or social activism to expose scheming politicians who use artifice to hold on to power. Fifthly, ivory tower intellectuals should avoid political co-option and use their knowledge to explain the eternal verities which are built into the various ideas so as to enhance the well-being of society. Finally, through biting satire and caricature, writers of fiction should unambiguously expose politicians' cunning and guile particularly in the way they polarise societies. For example, Ayi Kwei Armah's *The Beautiful Ones Are Not Yet Born* and Ngugi wa Thiong'o's *Devil on the Cross* are stinging satires on the how the post-colonial ruling elites, as well as the bourgeoisie, would thwart the dreams of the majority of the people. In the two works of fiction by the renowned novelist, both the ruling elites and the bourgeoisie in post-colonial, post-independence Africa were interested in filling the privileged positions which had been occupied by the colonialists whilst in power in Africa.

Chapter summary

During colonialism, and the resultant ensuing euphoria at the end of it, it can be said that the successes which African intellectuals achieved were in the domain of fighting against and bringing to an end colonial rule. However, from the end of colonial rule to the present, the political climate in Africa has always made the task of various categories of intellectuals (who wanted to make Africa work) quite challenging. In a word, with very few exceptions, the continent hardly produces a conducive political environment in which intellectual life could thrive, for any evidence of any intellectual climate was stifled before it got up. This sad state of affairs led to situations in which some effete intellectuals chose to yield to the lures of political power, whereas those "organic" intellectuals who were prepared to "speak truth to power" were either persecuted or hounded into exile, with the result that most dilemmas still remain unresolved. African intellectuals of various shades and hues need to be men and women of vision and high moral principles. They need to be progressive and forward-looking individuals who should work hard to instil such a spirit of dynamism in politicians. Thus, African intellectuals have a daunting task of exposing and challenging the decadence and moral degeneration of the ruling elites who think they have imperious entitlement to power while the majority of the populations wallow in despair because of ills such as ignorance (because of lack of education), hunger, and disease. African intellectuals should stand up to shoddy

The dilemmas of African intellectuals 49

political leadership which has left the African continent caught in all sorts of fears to do with ethnic tensions (and wars), genocides, and xenophobic attacks, as well as sluggish economic development and the failure of the values of democracy, human rights, and other related freedoms.

Note

1 Nesbitt explains and emphasises the types of dilemmas intellectuals were plunged into following the end of colonial rule in most African countries. Such predicaments made a good number of the intellectuals leave their counties for the Western world.

4 African intellectuals, culture, and decolonisation of knowledge

A dominant tradition in the historiography of the years following the end of colonial rule was that mostly black African intellectuals, such as writers of fiction and academics, began to make concerted attempts to define, or redefine, culture – the so-called African or "black" culture in terms of fixity and purity. They did this either through works of fiction or by simply trying to recoup pre-colonial cultures, which, so the argument went, colonialism denigrated and tried to annihilate. Black African intellectuals were to get set in their approach to the idea of culture, thereby becoming puritanical and orthodox because, as Sara Marzagora, has memorably asserted,

> [p]re-colonial African cultures were described as pure, static, uncontaminated, self-contained, a repository of authenticity to be rediscovered in the struggle to overcome colonial alienation. African historians attempted to decentre colonialism by showing the continuities between pre-colonial past and postcolonial present, and emphasizing African autonomy, agency an initiative prior to, and in the face of European advent.
>
> (2016: 163)

In other words, post-colonial black African intellectuals came up with an articulation of an African identity which was pure and fixed because it was linked to Africa's pre-colonial past. This would prompt black intellectuals, particularly in the domain of fiction-writing, to assume the role of examining not only national but also continental identity, by presenting the entire African continent as if it were a monoculture, meaning inhabited by only black people who share the same cultures and traditions. To that end, and for all sorts of reasons, notably nationalism, quite a number of such intellectuals had a vision of the so-called African culture as seen through rose-coloured spectacles whereby the identity of the African continent is synonymous with blackness, or the black race. As Sara Marzagora has further argued,

Culture and decolonisation of knowledge   51

while poststructuralism in Western Europe was "decentring" knowledge and language and rejecting the existence of a unified subject, nativism was a central component of African intellectual production. . . . In the perception of African thinkers . . . now that African states were finally independent it was necessary to recompose and reconstruct an autonomous and liberated African subjectivity.

(ibid: 161)

For most intellectuals at the time, the African continent was a monoculture. Consequently, barring a few exceptions, since the end of colonialism, most black African intellectuals who were working in the domain of Africa's cultural identity either tended increasingly to be identified with the idea of nativism or national cultures, by preaching the credo of "Africanness", or simply dabbled in debates of culture and identity in ways which presented the entire continent as having one monolithic, pure culture which is based on the black race. Put another way, most black intellectuals have shown little or no consideration for the fact that the African continent has always been home to people of other races. In this chapter, I make a case for the fact that such an approach to culture is constrained and limited by a fixation on racial identities on a continent where not only is there deep-seated hatred among the majority black people but also the cultures are as different as chalk from cheese. On such a continent of political divides which are largely engendered by issues such as ethnicity, religion, or other forms of identity, it does not matter even if politicians preach the idea of a pure African identity as if the continent is based on a monoculture. This is because "[n]ativism . . . is a major cause of violence, conflict and genocide in post-independence Africa" (ibid: 167). Thus, there is a need for African intellectuals who are so sensitive and refined that they are prepared to employ the kind of thinking, or logic, which transcends people's largely dissimilar outlooks on life in terms of cultural and religious beliefs, racial and ethnic identities, and ideological principles, as well as political affiliations.

For African intellectuals who preoccupied themselves with such discourses which emphasised the unity of Africa based on race, the idea of the so-called African culture was about the centrality of tradition and cultural values in opposition to the Western way of life. Such acts of paying homage to a culture which is seen as being monolithically black, authentic, and pure have been evident through movements such as the Negritude movement – a movement which remains a prime example of the kind of thinking according to which its exponents advocated and popularised the value of embracing native cultures. The Negritude movement sentimentalised and glamourised Africa's pre-colonial past and traditions, which, it was argued, needed to be recovered. But even so, there were some African intellectuals who would

52 *Culture and decolonisation of knowledge*

not share in such a view of cultural identity in the changing world. Thus, it is not surprising that, as Benita Parry has put it, Negritude has been

> routinely disparaged as the most exorbitant manifestation of a mystified ethnic essentialism, as an undifferentiated and retrograde discourse installing notions of a foundational and fixed native self and demagogically asserting the recovery of an immutable past.
>
> (1996: 91)

What Parry is hinting at is the fact that, since the idea of the Negritude introduces notions of essentialism, meaning emphasising the idea of pure black African identity, the Negritude movement has been scoffed at by some black African thinkers, or intellectuals, because it introduces the idea of Manicheanism, which is about notions of. Self and Otherness. One such intellectual who made a sneering comment on and disapproved of the Negritude movement was Ezekiel Mphahlele, a South African writer of fiction, who argued that the "Negritude as an artistic programme is unworkable for modern Africa" (1974: 84) precisely because its impulse revolves around a "rejection of the other" (ibid: 85). Thus, as an intellectual who was wary of such a baleful fascination with a pure African identity, Mphahlele calls into question a movement whose ideology is based on nothing but narcissism in its promotion of a pure African identity that is in opposition to other groups of people who occupy the same continent. For Mphahlele, such a nostalgia for an African past, to the exclusion of other races and traditions, is pointless as the past, of black African traditions, can hardly be recuperated, considering current technological advancement according to which the idea of identity formation cannot be intrinsically based on only particular traditions. Considering that the force of modernity is, say, in the form of Christianity, as well as technological advancement, in the form of social media, shows the fluid and layered nature of the identity of the African continent. Mphahlele was a typical intellectual whom current African intellectuals should emulate.

In recent times, particularly towards the end of the twentieth century, as well as in the first decade of the twenty-first century, some South African post-colonial, "post-apartheid" intellectuals have actively taken part in similar debates which play up notions of an essentialised (black) African identity through the promotion of notions of identity which are predicated on philosophies that revolve around and glamourise the notion of "blackness", or the black race. One such instance of overplaying ideas of blackness finds its articulation in Thabo Mbeki's somewhat controversial notion the African Renaissance – a philosophy which points to the idea of promoting exclusive cultures and identities which represent and mark out black

Culture and decolonisation of knowledge 53

people not just in South Africa but also across the African continent and the world as sharing the same identity. Foremost among such intellectuals is Thabo Mbeki – a man whose intellectual bent has not been restricted to the domains of just economics and politics but also includes culture. There is no denying that, as the second president of post-apartheid South Africa, Mbeki was a public intellectual of some repute. He is remembered as an intellectual particularly when one considers the facility with which he sometimes used to quote William Shakespeare during his political speeches or addresses to the nation – the kind of speeches in which he used to emphasise the importance of embracing universalism. During his presidency, South Africa in particular and the world at large saw the emergence of an intellectual who would give voice to a range of discourses, including, somewhat controversially, his contribution towards the discourse on HIV/AIDS – the kind of commentary which attracted the attention, and wrath, of quite a number of scientists who argued that Mbeki's understanding of the notion and nature of HIV/AIDS was partial, sketchy, and certainly wanting.

Having said that, as he was an insightful thinker, one could argue that Mbeki's enduring legacy, as far as cultural identity is concerned, is his conceptualisation and formulation of the vision of Africa through an appeal to so-called African tradition. Such an appeal was articulated in his "I Am an African" speech – a speech in which he promotes the idea of the African Renaissance as a vision in which he sees black Africans as having a special destiny on the African continent and in the world. In the "I Am an African" speech, Mbeki declares his identity in the expression "I . . . claim that I am an African" (1998: 32). In this pronouncement, there is no doubt that the word *African* is an unmistakable reference to the black people and race. This becomes evident when he proclaims his affiliation with other black ethnic tribes across the continent from Ethiopia through Sudan to Ghana, to mention a few examples. Such an affiliation is indicative of the fact that he feels anchored in the place or land of the black people. Then, as if making a turnaround, he deviates from the core of his argument in his comments on the South African constitution, saying that "[i]t is a firm assertion made by ourselves that South Africa belongs to all who live in it, black and white" (ibid: 34). Remarkably, these famous remarks by Mbeki are now part of the South African constitution and have been engraved in the minds of most South Africans irrespective of race or creed. That he pronounced his identity in terms of blackness (when South Africa and many African countries have multiple identities) shows the extent to which most black African intellectuals may well feel conflicted about culture and identity, in this case, African identity.

Yet again, in the "African Renaissance" speech, Mbeki's intellectual streak is evident when he announces that "Africa needs her renaissance"

54 *Culture and decolonisation of knowledge*

(ibid: 297). He asserts that this is important for reasons such as colonialism, as well as the failure of the post-colonial African state – the latter being the main reason – so he argues, for the damaging and invasive stereotypes which the African continent has suffered going back to the colonial times. Thus, he states that the African Renaissance is necessary because "colonizers sought to enslave and destroy the African soul" (ibid: 299) and so the renewal involves "a journey of self-discovery and restoration of our own self-esteem" (ibid: 300). Yet again, he seems to go off at a tangent by bemoaning the failure of democracy in those African countries where war is raging and black people are killing one another. He avers that

> the children of Africa, from north to South, from the east to the west and at the centre of our continent, continue to be consumed by death dealt out by those who have proclaimed a sentence of death on dialogue and reason and on the children of Africa, whose limbs are too weak to run away from the rage of the adults. Both these, the harbingers of death and the victims are as African as you and I.
>
> (ibid: 296)

> Neither has Africa any need for the petty gangsters who could be our governors by theft of elective positions as a result of holding fraudulent elections, or by purchasing positions of authority through bribery and corruption.
>
> (ibid: 297)

> The thieves and their accomplices, the givers of bribes and the recipients are as African as you and I.
>
> (ibid: 297)

> The African renaissance demands that we purge ourselves of the parasites and maintain a permanent vigilance against the danger of the entrenchment in African society of this rapacious stratum with its social morality according to which everything in society must be organized materially to benefit the few.
>
> (ibid: 298)

Here, Mbeki points to how black African leaders gloss over the complexity of what kind of continent Africa is and has been. That is why he reflects not only on the depredations of war and tyranny across the continent but also on the pervasiveness of corruption. In addition to colonialism, these excesses prompt him to call for and advocate the African Renaissance. The core of the renaissance involves an "all-round struggle to end poverty, ignorance

Culture and decolonisation of knowledge   55

and backwardness" (ibid: 299). For this to be accomplished, Mbeki envisions the return to Africa of all black African people with expertise in various fields, including those black African pundits who are plying their trade outside of the African continent. Mbeki states that such experts should return in order to "inquire into and find solutions to Africa's problems and challenges; to open the African door to the world of knowledge; to elevate Africa's place within the universe of research, the formation of new knowledge, education and information" (ibid: 299). For Mbeki, the idea of an African Renaissance, hence African identity, is predicated on racial blackness. As far as Mbeki's notion of the African Renaissance is concerned, Africa's advancement is only possible if all black people from around the world were to return to the continent and make a contribution towards its development. But the lingering question is apart from slavery, which caused a lot of black people to leave the African continent, why do so many black African people still want to leave Africa for the Western world? In fact, most black people who live in the Western world were forced into leaving the African continent by mostly black African politicians.

This explains why Mbeki's idea of African Renaissance has not been well received by some other intellectuals, particularly in the academe. For example, Joyce Mistry sees Mbeki's dream as a rather nostalgic cultural programme in which he envisions the entire African continent's renewal through a return to the past. As she has put it,

> [f]or Mbeki, the reawakening of an African past is a necessary means of redirecting cultural policy. It is not so much an effort of celebrating a multicultural . . . society as much as it is about reclaiming the lost traditions of a past African glory. Mbeki's objectives privilege African languages and African philosophy.
>
> (2001: 12)

Here, Mistry rightly points out that Mbeki sees so-called black African cultures as populist nostalgia, and that is why he demonstrates a longing for the past, instead of appreciating the fact that the criteria of cultural affinity and belonging are now fluid, contested, and contingent.

Another scholar who has also challenged Mbeki's idea of the African Renaissance is Natasha Distiller.[1] In a text known as *Shakespeare and the Coconuts: On Post-Apartheid South African Culture*, Distiller has called into question Mbeki's idea of the African Renaissance, saying it lacks articulation and is simply confined to generalities. Distiller's challenging of Mbeki's idea of the African Renaissance is based on a binary of "European and African" (2012: 133), a thinking in oppositional categories, according to which black Africans are seen as a homogeneous group of people whose

56 *Culture and decolonisation of knowledge*

apparently homogeneous and pure culture ought to be saved and protected, and yet Africa has always been a continent inhabited by people of various races. In particular, she challenges the ideological issue and focus of Thabo Mbeki's idea of the African Renaissance by showing how the name and its logic are predicated on the European Renaissance and its high culture and hence represents the idea of coconutness – the fluid and shifting idea of African identity. She states that definition of culture which is built into the idea the African Renaissance flies in the face of the idea of coconut identity, which is a hard reality not only in South Africa but also across the entire African continent, where the young generation are embracing what is evidently a liminal or hybrid identity. Hence, Distiller maintains that Mbeki's idea is not a well-thought-out one because it smacks of elitism and political opportunism and thus contributes very little towards the whole debate about identity politics. Basically, she sees Mbeki's articulation of the idea of the African Renaissance as being predicated on a paradigm of European history to reconceptualise and rework a romanticised, pure African culture and identity. For this reason, Distiller argues that the idea is based on a binary of "European" and "African", presenting people of black African origin as though they were a homogeneous group, though Africa has always had "others" in it. For Distiller, Mbeki's obsession with the idea of an African Renaissance becomes a form of narcissism and smacks of mere political opportunism. In a sense, Mbeki is a latter-day apostle of African culture while still largely admiring the West. Thus, Distiller suggests that Mbeki's idea of Africanness, as implied in the idea of the African Renaissance, becomes just a fetish, if not a quixotic ideological construct.

Both intellectuals, Mistry and Distiller, fault Mbeki's idea of the Renaissance for the homogenising effect of the discourse which suggests that it is rooted in and smacks of essentialism. In other words, in the "I Am an African" speech, he sets up binaries about "Africa" based on blackness and the Otherness of races. What the two scholars have in common is the ability to see Mbeki as being a partisan intellectual, instead of providing a disinterested pronouncement on notions of culture and identity across Africa. Even if black people are the majority, the reality is that Africa is a plural society, the notion of plurality coming from the fact that the continent is still home to people of many races.

However, in spite of the criticism, there is no doubt that Mbeki's philosophy of the African Renaissance places him among African intellectuals of great note. This is because as he theorises the notion of the African Renaissance, he takes cognisance of the fact that the continent is notorious for all forms of ills, notably perennial ethnic conflicts, which often lead to wars, disease, and hunger, to mention a few examples of the ills which harm the people of this continent. Thus, in the concept of the African Renaissance, he

Culture and decolonisation of knowledge 57

had a vision of a continent that needs to gradually move away from and dispense with such negative stereotypes and images that it has been notorious for going back to the colonial times. However, it is the homogeneous and essentialist readings of African culture and identity which rule Mbeki out from being regarded as a fully-fledged intellectual. This is because, owing to colonialism, there are various threads which define African identity, notably the presence of the autochthonous Khoisan (or Bushmen) people, the majority black people, whites, Indians, and Arabs. In the end, Mbeki points to the need for the continent to globalise, while, at the same time, the black people are reminded of their exclusive cultural identity. Crucially, as an intellectual, although he initially sets up binaries, he is clearly an advocate of a liminal position in which he sees the identity of South Africa, for instance, as a broad-based one in terms of the constitution, which accepted people of various races as South Africans. Such self-reflexivity of thought sets him apart as one of South Africa's admirable intellectuals of his generation.

Mbeki's bringing forth of the notion of the African Renaissance might well be seen as a phantom considering how different the twenty-first century is, as many black Africans have embraced various forms of modernity in the form of the Christian religion – Catholicism, Presbyterianism, and Pentecostalism. Further, Africans' embrace of consumerism leaves notions of a pure African identity as a mere misconception and misapprehension, which are largely fostered by some form of cheap romanticism.

How should African intellectuals perceive the idea of culture?

It would seem that, down the centuries, the idea of culture, in most societies, used to find expression in the kind of language which was largely categorical so as to show that culture was a pure and fixed category. For example, in Britain, Matthew Arnold's belief of culture was based on what he saw as a unique and typically British tradition. It was Raymond Williams who, in his text entitled *Culture and Society 1750–1950* (1958), called into question the Anordian idea of seeing culture as a pure and autonomous category. Williams's vision of culture would lead to the birth of the discipline of cultural studies – a field of study according to which the sense of the idea of culture has multiplied, as one can talk about popular cultures and subcultures.

Thus, the end of colonialism saw many black African intellectuals try to retrieve the so-called pre-colonial black African cultures, which colonialists used to denigrate and wanted to annihilate. However, it is very hard for post-colonial societies, including Africa, to define the idea of culture in terms of fixity when "[n]ativism, with its nostalgia for 'authentic' and 'pure' pre-colonial traditions, always got it wrong" (Marzagora

58 *Culture and decolonisation of knowledge*

2016: 167). This is partly because the light of modernity, say in the form of Christianity, continues to shine through most post-colonial societies, such as those in Africa. Further, with the realities of globalisation and technological progress, which largely define the modern world of the twenty-first century, the notion of culture is mostly a product of both the local and global dynamics. For example, through technology, most people from Africa are consumers of the global culture. This explains why in Chinua Achebe's archetypal African novel *Things Fall Apart*, while the protagonist is busy trying to pinpoint representations of local African culture, his son decides to join a Christian church. Little wonder that in an interview with Anthony Appiah in the 1990s, Achebe himself would state that "African identity is still in the making. There isn't a final identity that is African" (1992: 73). This entails that African intellectuals should avoid reducing the idea of the cultural identity of the entire African continent to pretentious localisation and purity, as if the whole continent is a monoculture. Rather, African intellectuals need to reflect on and think about the question of what it means to be an African in the globalised and globalising world of the twenty-first century, where the idea of culture is such a mobile way of life, it teaches us what it means to be human. As Homi Bhabha has put it,

> [t]he native intellectual who identifies the people with true national culture will be disappointed. The people are now the very principle of "dialectical reorganization" and they construct their cultures from the national text translated into modern Western forms of information technology, language, dress. The changed political and historical site of enunciation transforms the meaning of the colonial inheritance into the liberatory signs of a free people of the future.
>
> (2004: 55–56)

The gist of what Bhabha says in the preceding quotation is that, in the modern technologically driven and mediated world, intellectuals should take cognisance of the reality of identity formation as being no longer predicated on what are regarded as pure and original cultures. Thus, intellectuals have the obligation to provide direction in society with regard to notions of changing cultures and traditions – the kinds of changes which point to the fact that, in the changing world of the twenty-first century, identity – be it personal, cultural, national, or continental – is always in a state of transition. As Giroux has put it, "intellectuals need to recognise the limits of a politics based exclusively on theories of difference and identity" (2002: 399). In other words, intellectuals should avoid thinking of culture in terms of dualities, or binary oppositions. Further, Giroux states that

Culture and decolonisation of knowledge 59

intellectuals need a new discourse for grasping the unity of the social, political, and global community, not so much as to shut down a proliferation of identities based on theories of differences but to engage them through relations of solidarity engaged in broader struggles that reveal both the strengths and limits of such particularities.

(ibid: 399)

He goes on to assert that there is "the need to construct a democratic politics that affirms differences that matter but at the same time moves beyond a politics of limited interest groups" (ibid: 399). In other words, rather than think about and present the idea of culture in terms of difference, or Otherness of categories such as race, gender, sexuality, and other categories, intellectuals should take the idea of culture questioningly and provisionally. On the African continent, in particular, it is important to think about the confluence of identities that has been the distinguishing feature of the African continent for some millennia. Bhabha has also underlined the full import of the disposition of disinterestedness in intellectual pursuits by presenting or portraying "the committed intellectual as the theoretician of practical knowledge whose defining criterion is rationality and whose project is to combat the irrationality of ideology" (2004: 44).[2] In echoing Sartre, Bhabha argues that intellectuals should be highly perceptive when dealing with cultures and traditions, particularly if such cultures are linked to notions of holism or fixity. In this case, it stands to reason for African intellectuals to try to cultivate and maintain the spirit of neutrality and detachment as far as matters of culture and identity are concerned. This is because, rather than being immutable, there is always a level of dynamism in cultures and traditions, which makes them fluid and vibrant. Thus, it is only logical and pragmatic that perceptions about and reflections on African identity are based on confluences (of identities), namely the first nations, such as the Khoisan, the Malays, black and African, Arab and African, Asian and African, and white and African, among others. After all, as the voice of conscience, intellectuals are typical philosophers who ought to show the link between ideas and social reality.

Decolonisation of knowledge

In recent years, there has been the emergence of decoloniality, or the discourse which is about the need to decolonise knowledge from what is portrayed as Eurocentric frames of reference. Often linked with largely Latino-American scholars such as Anibal Quijano, Walter Mignolo, Ramon Grosfoguel, Enrique Dussel, and Nelson Maldonaldo Torres, to name a few examples, decolonial scholars perceive most forms of knowledge in the

60   *Culture and decolonisation of knowledge*

world as being fundamentally Eurocentric and therefore worth destabilising and deconstructing so that post-colonial societies can come up with parallel forms of knowledge which are based on local cultures and histories. For example, Mignolo argues that the notion of decolonising knowledge is about the need to "de-link from eurocentrism" (Mignolo, in Isasi-Diaz & Mendieta 2012: 23). For Grosfoguel, decolonising knowledge is about calling into question "the epistemological myth of Eurocentered modernity" (2012: 89), meaning deconstructing the idea of modernity which, it is assumed, constitutes only Eurocentric knowledge.

In a different context, in a text entitled *Provincializing Europe*, Dipesh Chakrabarty has shown the extent to which various temporalities in post-colonial societies co-exist and coincide with the time of Western modernity. Chakrabarty goes on to argue that such a coexistence can be used as a tool for deconstructing Western teleological time, including the various forms of modernities which are rendered visible in different forms, such as capitalist globalisation. Finally, in his text entitled *African Intellectuals and Decolonization*, Nicholas Creary talks about the need to have "the struggle to decolonize African knowledge and the roles that Africa and Africanist intellectuals play in this . . . struggle" (2012: 3). He goes on to argue that this is significant because "African voices have a right to be heard within intellectual discourses and a responsibility to represent themselves within intellectual discourses" (ibid: 3). What these scholars mean by decolonising knowledge is the ability to analyse, review, and rework what is seen as Western knowledge so that it is bereft, or disposed, of any Eurocentric undertones of universalism. The aim of getting post-colonial societies to decolonise Western knowledge is to come up with versions of knowledge whose cannons of understanding relate to local histories, cultures, and traditions. The assumption is that it is local, post-colonial (or decolonial) intellectuals who would revise and re-work the Western knowledge so that it reflects local cultures and ways of life. As a practice, decoloniality largely makes use of Frantz Fanon's approach to challenging colonialism, as well as drawing on the Foucauldian genealogical method – a paradigm of archaeology which is a theoretical framework for analysing discourses in society. It deals with the discourse of "coloniality" and the construction of new forms of knowledge.

How should African and Africanist intellectuals perceive the notion of decolonising knowledge?

That all forms of knowledge in society should be subject to examination and interrogation is something incontrovertible. In the past, Africa has had men and women of unquestionable conscience who have questioned and challenged all kinds of knowledge, particularly colonialism. For example,

Culture and decolonisation of knowledge 61

during the years when South Africa was under the apartheid regime, both black and white Africanists decolonised the discourse of apartheid with such vivid imagination until the practice was brought to an end. This is because it was easy to decolonise the clear-cut process of colonialism whose distinguishing feature was the idea of difference, or Othering. In other words, at the core of colonial discourse was the notion of identity (of white and black races), which was based on binary oppositions.

Having said that, like culture, the idea of decolonising all forms of knowledge requires the kinds of intellectuals who are broad-minded and well-informed individuals whose approach to the notion of decolonisation, particularly in the twenty-first century, is informed by well-thought-out perceptions about the nature of knowledge, as well as knowledge production. Such individuals ought to be champions of conscience in society because, in thinking about decolonising knowledge, African intellectuals should develop an awareness of the fact that societies tend to be defined and characterised by various forms of hierarchies, some of which are inimical to people's lives, notably patriarchy. For example, there are certain forms of knowledge which either teach and promote universal ideals or present the fluid and shifting nature of human identity, say, through culture. Any questioning of such categories of knowledge requires the application of conscience and prudence. For instance, the idea of decolonising knowledge is anything but a new epistemology. Decolonising knowledge remains a rebarbative and unsavoury framework for thinking about identity in the twenty-first century, because as a form of adversarial politics, it amounts to navel-gazing. It is a form of orthodoxy which introduces the idea of Manicheanism, meaning representations of human identity which are based on binaries or oppositional categories. In any case, post-colonial countries, especially in Africa, are notorious for what Pheng Cheah calls the "betrayal of the egalitarian ideals of anticolonial revolution and the rapid onset of neocolonialism", which "have cast a grave doubt on the continuing viability of the teleological time of decolonization" (2016: 198).

What is striking about what Cheah says is the fact that, since the end of colonialism, the ruling elites have thwarted the dreams of the majority of the populations. This is because, in the post-colonial, post-independence era,

> the bourgeois national project of modernity relies on modern state and civil society inherited from the colonial regime to exclude, silence and exploit the subaltern sectors of the population.
>
> (ibid: 202)

Once colonialism was over, the middle class of most post-colonial states became only interested in filling the privileged positions that were occupied

62 *Culture and decolonisation of knowledge*

by the colonial power, this at the expense of the entire population, which was subject to all forms of exclusion. If the ruling elites and the bourgeois in post-colonial societies are only interested in making themselves happy, then the idea of decolonising knowledge amounts to a tunnel vision on the part of decolonial scholars in terms of where to take the post-colonial world.

Further, Gregory McLennan has questioned decolonial scholars' rejection of the notion of universalism as unthinkable. As he has put it,

> it is not necessarily the case, epistemologically speaking, that all aspects of universalism . . . are thereby condemned, either as plain wrong or as definitely Eurocentric.
>
> (2013: 137)

He goes on to state that the notion of "modernity is indispensable because it can hardly be denied" (ibid: 137). The core of McLennan's argument is interesting in the sense that it is indeed difficult to decolonise some forms of knowledge which are cross-cultural in nature, notably Christianity, which is of Semitic origins, as well as arithmetical expressions, such as Roman and Arabic numerals. These are stimulating instances which render the idea of universalism as not being simply Eurocentric but multicultural.

Remarkably, in the 1980s, three Nigerian intellectuals of literary bent, namely Chinweiuzu, Jemie, and Madubuike, published a book entitled *Toward the Decolonization of African Literature* – a text in which they argued for the privileging of the idea of nativism in African literature. These scholars wanted black African writers of fiction to re-think the idea of literary aesthetics so as to introduce the notion of Afrocentricism, or the promotion of the idea of black African identity across the African continent. For them, African literature was to be defined in terms of African orality and local customs, cultures, and traditions. The idea was to decolonise knowledge so that the literature from the African continent would emphasise, pinpoint, and reflect notions of black African personality and image. Convinced about Afrocentric particularism, the scholars were aiming for the deconstruction of the idea of Eurocentrism, also seen as universalism in literature, so that African literature could be aligned with notions of black African cultures, nationalism, and Pan-Africanism. One wonders if these scholars had any awareness about the work of Cheik Anta Diop, who, in his work entitled *The African Origin of Civilization: Myth or Reality*, demonstrated the extent to which what is regarded as Western civilisation was not purely European in nature. As I have put it in Chapter 6, Diop saw what is seen as European civilisation and knowledge as not being exclusively European. Further, it was top-notch intellectual Frantz Fanon, who, in his famous text *Black Skin, White Masks*, had already portrayed with prescience

Culture and decolonisation of knowledge 63

the fact that post-colonial African leaders would thwart the dreams of their people, with the middle class interested in filling the privileged positions which were occupied by the colonial power. It is not surprising that, since the emergence of the discourse of decolonisation in literary studies in the 1980s, this discourse has undercut itself because, as far as notions of aesthetics and themes are concerned, most writers of fiction continue to use Western frames of reference, as well as global themes, which reflect African identity not as unique but rather in terms of quotidian existence with regard to the continent's link with the world. As Madhu Khrishnan has put it, the third generation of African literature, that is from the 1990s to date, is such that the writers "have been heralded for their questioning of determined identity markers" (2013: 74) and "mirroring a larger global tendency in the postcolonial and African novel" (ibid: 74). Thus, Khrishnan goes on to pinpoint the main themes of current African fiction as "contemporary notions of cosmopolitanism, globalization, nomadism and liminality" (ibid: 74). It is such intellectuals as Cheik Diop, Frantz Fanon, and Madhu Khrishnan that other African intellectuals should get their impetus from as far as the notion of decolonising knowledge is concerned. Further, the rejection of universalism collapses in the light of the fact that what are seen as some aspects of universal knowledge, notably Roman and Arabic numerals (in mathematics) and Christianity (which is of Semitic origins), resonate with not only the notion of Eurocentrism but also the idea of universalism, which reflects the multicultural nature of knowledge. This leaves the idea of decolonisation of knowledge in the twenty-first century an essentialising discourse which caters to all kinds of stereotypes in categories such as race, gender, sexuality, religion, and other categorisations.

Yet again, African intellectuals need to be judicious and circumspect when it comes to reflecting on the idea of decolonising knowledge in the post-colonial societies, such as those in Africa, where most people struggle to meet needs such as food, shelter, education, and health care. An African intellectual should be able to show the extent to which the discourse of decolonisation points to the initiation of real change in society, or it is simply an anachronism. African intellectuals should be able to pinpoint the grey areas which decolonial scholars either take for granted or that elude them. Intellectuals cannot unthinkingly accept the idea of decolonisation, which introduces the adversarial politics of Self and Other, or identity politics – a politics which set in motion Frantz Fanon's notion of Manicheanism, whereby the notion of identity is based on the idea of difference or Otherness. For example, decolonial scholars' deconstruction of the idea of universalism undermines the role of the humanities, which have always been at the service of a common humanity. Thus, intellectuals need to bear in mind the fact that any obsession with the idea of culture and decolonisation

64 *Culture and decolonisation of knowledge*

of knowledge tends to yield the reality of co-option by politicians. Since the end of colonialism, one can argue that the problem of Africa is not what is regarded as Eurocentric knowledge.

Chapter summary

With regard to the idea of culture in Africa, black African intellectuals' proclivity for pure national and continental cultures is inconceivable considering the various races of people who inhabit the continent. Culture is a social construct. Further, as a socio-political and cultural approach to interrogating the discourse of colonialism, the discourse of decolonisation has to be examined and fully contextualised so as to determine if it is the key factor to address all sorts of problems in post-colonial societies, particularly in Africa. The reality is that the theory falls short on many counts. On a continent where issues such as ethnicity, religion, and sexuality spark off all kinds of problems and antagonistic politics of binary thinking in terms of race, ethnicity, gender, nationalism, and other categories, the discourse of decolonising knowledge simply introduces adversarial politics. The discourse clearly circumvents the reality of our times, which reflects the idea of universalism and what it means to be human.

Notes

1 Distiller faults Thabo Mbeki's notion of the African Renaissance for not being thought through.
2 Bhabha here echoes the ideas of Sartre on intellectuals.

5 Taking a leaf from the Western intellectual

The fact that African intellectuals should learn an object lesson from Western intellectuals does not mean that there are no former and current intellectuals of the African, or Africanist, milieu from whom African intellectuals can also draw some object lessons about the role of a black African intellectual. The fact is that, as I indicate in Chapter 6, in the last fifty or so years, Africa has seen the emergence of a number of African intellectuals, notably politicians, artists, and writers of fiction, who demonstrated a great deal of lateral thinking in the way they perceived and tackled various problems in their societies across the African continent. But then, one wonders why Africa is still largely defined in terms of social ills, such as ethnic conflicts, corruption, patronage, the lack of democracy, and other related freedoms. This state of affairs suggests the continent does not have enough progressive and enterprising intellectuals to fight several bleak political establishments.

Basically, by introducing Western intellectuals as paragons of philosophy or thinkers whom African intellectuals should emulate, I am not trying to put the former on a pedestal vis-à-vis the ability and competence of the latter. Rather, the issue is that, down the centuries, the West has always had the perennial and long-standing tradition of producing the kind of thinkers who have interrogated all forms of knowledge in their societies. For example, just as the Renaissance period saw a number of intellectuals who worked on the rebirth of various forms of knowledge, the Enlightenment modernity, which was seen as the apotheosis of knowledge production, also engendered a number of intellectuals who questioned particular aspects of modernity, hence the discourse "was met with resistance from some philosophers . . . who held fast to ideas of universal humanity united by given capacity for meaning and civil life" (Spencer 2014: 43). Further, as opposed to most post-colonial countries, the flourishing of democracy in the West has always meant that a great deal of human rights and other related freedoms are upheld in the Western societies because a lot of issues about identity are subject to systematic debates and deep consideration. This explains why

66   *Taking a leaf from the Western intellectual*

each time Western political leaders fall short in their vision of how to run their country or society, Western intellectuals of various shades are often resolute to attack and castigate such leaders for their flawed vision. Thus, I introduce the Western intellectual as a model thinker whom African intellectuals should pattern themselves after so that they can tenaciously and unflinchingly face the daunting vocation of navigating between the Scylla of colonialism, especially the formal one which is now largely over, and the Charybdis of ethnic tensions and wars and religious prejudices, as well as the failure of democracy and other freedoms – thorny issues which should be dealt with by African intellectuals of various types in this century.

In spite of the fact that democracy is the only tried-and-tested form of government globally, there is a great deal that African intellectuals can learn from the Western world. Granted, there is no doubt that the relevance and application of the notion of democracy has been in question in some Western countries. However, as a representative system of government, the system of democracy has, on the whole, thrived and succeeded in many Western countries, quite in opposition to what happens in most post-colonial countries, where, because of politicians' thinking that they are entitled to power, democracy is seen as if it is peripheral to their societies' needs. With some exceptions, the measure of such success in the Western world is the uptake and application of democratic ideals and values, something which is usually evident during the times of changeover of power from one political party to the next. Such an inclination of smooth and seamless transitions in most Western societies is a rare occurrence in Africa. With the overwhelming reality of the twenty-first century centred on or revolving around issues such as human rights, liberal democracy, globalisation, and technological advances, Africa needs a brand of intellectuals who are typically avant-garde thinkers from various domains of knowledge and who will help to transform a continent which is largely retrogressive to make some progress in various spheres of life. This is why my argument is that African intellectuals' vocation ought to mirror that of the Western ones, who are not only prepared to anatomise all forms of discourse but also quite primed to "speak the truth to power", to use Edward Said's expression.

Experience has also shown that Western political leaders are not immune to excesses, such as corruption, distortions, or obfuscation of information – the kinds of abuses or manipulations which are often associated with political power. Remarkably, each time a Western leader, especially of a presumably powerful democracy, was engaged in a political act which was deemed disingenuous in the sense of serving the interests of the politician, intellectuals in those countries – located either in the academe or the wider society – were set and primed to expose such abuses of power. In other words, be it an "ivory tower" or any educated "rank-and-file" thinker, the West has always

Taking a leaf from the Western intellectual   67

turned out rational and lucid intellectuals whose interests have lain in currents of thought which reflect the changing times and exigencies of their societies. On a regular basis, intellectuals have helped politicians to break free of the kinds of theories and schools of thought which constitute essentialising discourses on issues such as race, gender, religion, and democracy, to mention a few examples. Way back in the 1960s, for instance, Noam Chomsky was able to delineate and clarify the unique responsibilities of the Western intellectual as follows:

> Intellectuals are in a position to expose the lies of governments, to analyze actions according to their causes and motives and often hidden intentions. In the Western world, at least, they have the power that comes from political liberty, from access to information and freedom of expression. . . . Western democracy provides the leisure, facilities and the training to seek the truth lying hidden behind the veil of distortion and misrepresentation, ideology and class interest, through which the events of current history are presented to us. The responsibilities of intellectuals . . . are much deeper than the "responsibility of the people," given the privileges that intellectuals enjoy.
>
> (1967: 1)

For Chomsky, political life is never short of all manner of transgressions, which includes perversion or misrepresentation of truth by the ruling elites. Thus, Chomsky shows that the role of Western intellectuals is to ensure that politicians do not do whatever they want without being halted or punished. Hence, post-colonial societies, especially African countries, need to groom intellectuals as the kind of individuals who are regarded to have cultivated a moral consciousness which helps them to lay bare such political misdeeds that are a way of life for most African ruling elites. Interestingly, as an academic intellectual of great wisdom and moral awareness, not only was Chomsky against the Vietnam War, but he has often consistently spoken out against American aggressive foreign policies which led to unnecessary wars in the Western world. For working in the university as an expert in the field of his speciality, namely linguistics, as well as acting as a public figure in defence of the values of peace and justice in America, he combines all the qualities of a typically academic intellectual worth emulating. Africa needs to have intellectuals such as Chomsky because of the pervasiveness of tribulations such as wars, genocides, xenophobic attacks, and other forms of black-on-black violence – something which most African political leaders connive at or shut their eyes to. There are other kinds of ills, such as sluggish economic development, as well as the failure of any accomplishments in the spheres of democracy, human rights, and other related freedoms. All

68   *Taking a leaf from the Western intellectual*

these problems should be a wake-up call for African intellectuals when it comes to playing the role of having or maintaining the initiative to help the citizenry have life-enhancing experiences, such as good education, human rights, and other freedoms.

In the last fifty years or so, the influence of Western intellectuals such as Noam Chomsky has been nothing but phenomenal. For example, before Antonio Gramsci came onto the scene in the middle of the twentieth century, the idea and meaning of the word *intellectual* was largely delimited or circumscribed. As I have indicated in Chapter 1, for Gramsci, the meaning of an intellectual was to be understood in different senses to include what he termed *traditional intellectuals* – a broad category of people in society, including teachers and priests, who, although located outside of the domain of academia and knowledge production, still make a contribution to society in terms of carrying out functions such as explaining ideas like culture, as well as other generalised duties of social importance, notably the promotion of notions of liberalism. But the type of Western intellectual who has made a lasting impact is largely the "organic" one, or the kind of thinker in the Gramscian mould who is expected to step in and intercede whenever things go wrong in society. To that end, Julien Benda also stands out as one of the most prominent intellectuals in the first half of the twentieth century. In one of his major works, Benda bears witness to the moment of truth for modernity through the perverted ethics of intellectual life in the first part of the twentieth century. He exposes such a crisis of modernity in his seminal text *The Betrayal of the Intellectuals*. In this text, Benda exposes what he sees and describes as the treachery and pretensions of intellectuals. Writing about such a betrayal, he observed in his day how

> all the "clerks" have adopted political passions. No one will deny that throughout Europe to-day the immense majority of men of letters and artists, a considerable number of scholars, philosophers, and "ministers" of the divine share in the chorus of hatreds among races and political factions. Still less will be denied that they have adopted political passions.
>
> (1955: 31)

Here, Benda was deeply concerned about the rise of political passions in Europe in the form of nationalism, racism, and anti-Semitism. He bemoans the fact that, as intellectuals, his contemporaries had so aligned themselves with politics that the Second World War has always been infamous for the Holocaust. He thus denounced the intellectuals for embracing such damaging obsessions. For Benda, by aligning themselves with particular sentiments about nationalism and racism, to the detriment of universal

Taking a leaf from the Western intellectual 69

values, the intellectuals had betrayed their trust in the world, as representatives of change in society. To extrapolate Benda's ideas from Europe to Africa, with the exception of very few African countries where democracy works, most African political leaders suffer from all sorts of weaknesses, notably greed, intransigence, and impetuosity, as well as being impervious to criticism, no matter how constructive it may be. This explains why there have always been various instances of woes in Africa, particularly those to do with black-on-black violence.

These views expressed by Benda have also been echoed by Sara Danielsson. In her article entitled "The Intellectual as an Architect and Legitimizer of Genocide: Julien Benda Redux", she traces a pattern in the Europe of the first part of the twentieth century when Benda was always criticising intellectuals for "their corrupting political involvement" (2005: 396).[1] Put another way, she argues that what prompted Benda to denounce and condemn the intellectuals was the way they had lost their moral authority by prioritising politics over morality, with the result that Europe would be subjected to the evils of totalitarianism and racism – two major human vices which cast a blight on the twentieth century and, in a way, contributed to two world wars. Remarkably for Benda, while the century produced intellectuals most of whom aided and abetted the genocides during the Second World War (through operating in collusion with dictators such as Adolf Hitler and Joseph Stalin), so far, he is the one intellectual whose moral pathos remains unparalleled and unequalled in the West, precisely because he reminded fellow intellectuals to be at the forefront of telling politicians to avoid essentialising discourses which were linked to power. Benda pinpoints the intellectuals' collusion with politicians through his observation of the way in which leftist intellectuals helped dictators such as Joseph Stalin to stay in power, just as rightist intellectuals also propped up Adolf Hitler in Germany, the kind of support for politicians which had serious consequences in the Holocaust during the Second World War. Thus, it would be interesting to see the lives and careers of twenty-first-century African intellectuals patterned on humanist Julien Benda – an intellectual of consummate rationality and wisdom who underscored in his philosophy the primacy of morality over cheap politicking. Africa needs intellectuals of courage and vision so that, like Benda, they remind politicians to have the obligation to discharge the kinds of responsibilities which are linked to notions of truth and social justice.

Apart from Benda's contribution, the second part of the twentieth century will be remembered for the development of one scholarly movement which has come to be known as the linguistic turn – an evolution in European continental philosophy which would lead to new ways of thinking about knowledge and identity. According to this movement, the whole idea of

70 *Taking a leaf from the Western intellectual*

identity, including that of the self, is fashioned or produced through a never-ending play of language. Although there are various names associated with this development, only a few are worth examining, namely Michel Foucault and Jacques Derrida. Michel Foucault is probably the most remarkable intellectual to have come out in the second half of the twentieth century. He demonstrated the primacy of language in identity politics, pointing out the extent to which notions of cultures and selves are produced through a process in which discourse reflects a continuous process in which language is performed.

As one of the most powerful and influential thinkers of the twenty-first century, Foucault looked at archaeology, or the nature of discourse, and pinpointed the fact that one cannot divorce the circumstances of knowledge production from power. What Foucault did was to historicise and contextualise the different kinds of "truth" located in what was seen as knowledge, rationality, and reason which had developed in various cultures. Then, he came up with the notion of epistemes as being central to various ideas about knowledge. For Foucault, the organising principle around such forms of knowledge was the notion of what he termed *episteme*s – ideas which were also based on what he termed *discursive formations*, meaning, "a field of statement and textual events that reflect relations of social-cultural power" (Castle 2007: 310). Many such formations are "structured hierarchically and reinforce established traditions and dominant ideologies" (ibid: 310). They are also "characterized . . . by the creation of rules of exclusion and, to this extent, are self-regulating systems" (ibid: 310). In short, Foucault demonstrated that knowledge, or what are seen as various forms of truth, are not essential and ahistorical. Rather, they are produced by *epistemes*, or linked to the way in which power is exercised. As far as the idea of knowledge is concerned, African intellectuals need to learn from such pre-eminent Western intellectuals as Foucault. This is because, for him, it is epistemes which organise thought and make various forms of knowledge appear as if they are categorical imperatives or absolute truths. He went on to state that epistemes make sense through what he termed discursive formations, that is, particular statements or pronouncements, which show the link between knowledge and power. In other words, epistemes, which are often rendered visible through discursive formations, are the shaping or organising principles around the idea of knowledge.

Thus, in order to challenge various forms of knowledge, Foucault came up with the notion of discourse as being built into the idea of knowledge. By discourse, Foucault meant a regime of thought which is seen as having particular claims to truth. He went on to state that, since knowledge is often associated with people who wield power, it is such people who embrace particular discourses and aim to impose any of such discourses'

Taking a leaf from the Western intellectual 71

schemes of classification on the social world. In short, discourse points to the ways in which power in society is constituted. What makes Foucault an archetypal intellectual is his ability and preparedness to examine and honour gaps and silences in discourses. When he applied his thinking to the nature of Enlightenment modernity, he carried out the task with such facility that he made a lasting contribution towards a gradual transformation of society. Foucault's exploration of the hegemonic power of discourse made him claim that knowledge and truth are linked in the way power is exercised in society. His main and unique contribution in the domains of the humanities remains his engagement with the concept of power, particularly regarding the way in which rulers often use it to dominate the ruled, or their subjects. To that end, Foucault introduces the idea of discourse – a notion which, simply defined, refers to a regime of thought which is seen to have particular claims to truth. Foucault goes on to argue that it is often those who wield power who come up with the notion of discourse and begin to impose its schemes of classification on the social world, seeing such truths as categorical imperatives. Thus, concepts such as the universal institution of patriarchy, race, ethnicity, sexuality, religion, and other related forms of knowledge which underscore the idea of exclusive identities are a result of the prevalence of discourses in society. Foucault had reached such an understanding of discourse following his determined effort to historicise and contextualise what were seen as various kinds of truth, knowledge, and rationality which had developed in societies and cultures. In the end, he challenged what were seen as "absolutist" and teleological notions which were built into such forms of knowledge.

Jacques Derrida is another intellectual whose philosophical thinking is at odds with modernity's representation of reality as being nothing but transcendence. A philosopher of the idea of deconstruction, Derrida sees the slippery and skidding nature of language as being one of the reasons why our world remains a never-ending, shifting system of meanings, and thus the existence of notions of objective knowledge may well be impractical. In other words, the notion of deconstruction enables a humbling awareness of the fact that whatever truth we talk about is not absolute or conclusive. Derrida's work has energised and galvanised intellectual inquiry well beyond the purview of the philosophical tradition. Not only did Derrida use the notion of deconstruction to draw attention to the limits of thought, but he also went on to use his deconstructive technique to challenge particular hierarchies in the Western world which seemed to lay claim to historicity. It is not surprising that Derrida's work has been used as a profound challenge to Western ethnocentrism, with his idea of deconstruction being applied to decolonise and destabilise European thought, particularly modernity's use of race as a category for defining identity. Further, the idea of deconstruction

72 *Taking a leaf from the Western intellectual*

has been applied to disciplines such as law and politics to demonstrate the limits of some of the discourses in these fields.

Both Foucault and Derrida are the kind of intellectuals whom African intellectuals need to learn from with regard to the ideas of discourse and deconstruction, which shed light on notions of race, ethnicity, and identity. In particular, the notion of discourse is pertinent to the issue of what African identity is about or entails. This is because, for centuries now, the African continent has been inhabited by people of various races. Hence, the discourse of African identity needs to be re-examined.

As far as the idea of culture is concerned, an intellectual of great vision was a British scholar known as Raymond Williams, "one of the founders of British Cultural Studies" (Castle 2007: 215). Williams will always be remembered as a top-notch British intellectual because while, over the years, the idea of British culture had been perceived from Matthew Arnold's notion of seeing culture as a totality and, hence, "a coherent and self-regulating tradition" (ibid: 72), Williams would challenge this view of culture by coming up with "an alternative vision that recognizes the dynamism and complexity of late-capitalist society, the web-like connections that link subcultures and the various class formations within overlapping regional and national frameworks" (ibid: 72). For Williams, culture is not an autonomous and fixed entity but a social construct.

Apart from being a pure Western intellectual, Edward Said was a Palestinian intellectual who was based in the West and used to think like a typical Western intellectual. This is because he was intensely and truly attuned to the needs of not just his countrymen and women but also the entirety of humankind. Thus, Said also remains preeminent amongst the crop of intellectuals of his generation in that, besides carrying out works of scholarship at Columbia University in the USA – the kind of work in which he was sui generis and excelled with exemplary facility – he also remained a truly engaged intellectual with respect to nurturing public discourse and promoting change not just in America but also the wider world, including Palestine, his native country. In other words, his life was a consistent demonstration or proof of what it means to be a public intellectual with moral authority. Thus, over and above his active involvement in academic life, he rendered visible his non-partisan streak of an "organic" intellectual by giving a running commentary on issues of politics in America and Israel, as well as his native country of Palestine. For example, he is known to have inveighed against the political brinkmanship of America, just as he was critical not only of "Israel's flouting of international laws and its repeated affronts to human dignity" (Varadharajan 2013: 62) but also of corruption and intimations of political immaturity within the Palestinian Liberation Organisation (PLO). Thus, although he was a scholar, or a member of the intelligentsia, he was

Taking a leaf from the Western intellectual 73

also an "organic" intellectual, or a real productive thinker, who used to give voice to crucial issues in society, both globally and in Palestinian society.

As for writers of fiction, George Orwell was one of the most powerful Western intellectuals in that he was a fiction writer, as well as a literary examiner and critic. For example, in his famous allegorical novel *Animal Farm*, Orwell evidently satirises Stalinism by challenging class and political ideologies. Then he went on to examine *Gulliver's Travels* – a text which has representations of war and disease. In his essay "Politics Versus Literature: An Examination of *Gulliver's Travels*", Orwell demonstrates his total dissatisfaction with the politics of the day, particularly totalitarianism, which had led to the Second World War.

Finally, as a journalist, Bill Bryson stands out as one of the most influential Western intellectuals today. Not only has Bryson worked as a journalist in Britain and America; he has also published books about almost every continent, including Africa. Having worked for the *Times* newspaper (in Britain) and the *New York Times* (in the USA), Bryson has published books such as *Notes from a Small Island* (about Britain), *The Lost Continent: Travels in Small Town America* (the USA), *Down Under* (Australia), and *Bill Bryson's African Diary* (about Africa). In all these books, Bryson delivers descriptions, reflections, and comical and satirical musings about the various societies he has been to. Of course, Bryson's *A Short History of Nearly Everything* is an immensely interesting book in which his thinking about reflections on knowledge and life in general cut across various disciplines and spheres of life.

How African intellectuals' work should match that of Western intellectuals

African intellectuals' mission in life can easily mirror the sense of vocation which particular Western intellectuals have demonstrated in the last few centuries only if the intellectuals from across the African continent choose to become independent thinkers who are prepared to develop a spirit of goodwill, as well as a great awareness of the nature of knowledge in society. Since there are various spectra and horizons of experience in life which demand human attributes such as intelligence, confidence, outspokenness, pragmatism, and open-mindedness, to mention a few clear-cut and useful intellectual traits, Africa needs the kind of intellectuals who are broad-minded enough to deal with various forms of knowledge, as well as experiences, in the realms of both the natural sciences and the humanities. African intellectuals should avoid any enticement to uncritically embrace discourses, particularly in fields of knowledge such as race, gender, sexuality, nationality, religion, and other classifications – spheres of knowledge

74 *Taking a leaf from the Western intellectual*

which need a great deal of debate or exchange of views. African intellectuals should be alive to the reality of the generally unremarkable lives of African politicians, particularly those who are men or women of no vision. For example, some politicians introduce into political discourses notions such as populism and ideology, and yet all that they are interested in is power. Some politicians demand absolute fealty from the citizens but hardly work toward making the entire population happy and satisfied with their rule. For the African continent to achieve progress, after Foucault, African intellectuals should be prepared to question what are presented as "absolutist" and essentialist versions of human activities, ideas, and meanings.

Chapter summary

Western intellectuals are the kinds of philosophers whose insights into various forms of knowledge, such as science, politics, ideology, culture, and identity, have always helped their societies to make meaningful advancement, or progress, in many spheres of life. In fact, the West has produced the kind of thinkers whose impacts have been felt globally. To that end, it is vitally important that, for African intellectuals, there are a great many lessons to learn from Western intellectuals such as Julien Benda, Michel Foucault, and Noam Chomsky, whose abilities to think critically make them the enemies of all forms of extremism in society. Africa is a continent with mostly the kind of politicians who use a piecemeal approach to dealing with and addressing problems in their societies. Thus, like the West, the continent needs the kind of intellectuals who should provide penetrating criticism of what they see happening in their societies – societies which suffer from economic and social malaise.

Note

1 Sara Danielsson demonstrates the extent to which Western intellectual Julien Benda was able to decry the corrupting role of those Western intellectuals in the first half of the twentieth century who reneged on their roles (of standing for justice and truth) by yielding to the temptation of what he called ruling passions of state, class, and race – the kinds of passions which contributed to the outbreak of the First World War in which the notion of race was at the core.

6 A paradigm of an African intellectual in the twenty-first century

In this chapter, rather than leaving the reader with lingering doubts as to whether the African continent has the potential to transform, I posit a model of intellectuals of different races and calibres from the African continent who have been in the vanguard of change in the past as the standard of perfection which should be embraced. Through the promotion of soul-searching about notions such as politics, identity, and culture, some of these intellectuals have demonstrated the kind of initiative which has helped the citizenry of societies of which they are part to know and attain life-enhancing experiences, including human rights and other related freedoms. Talking about freedom, Ben Okri has stated that

> we are all still learning how to be free.
> Freedom is the beginning of the greatest possibility of human genius.
>
> (1997: 132)

The reality of what Okri avers in the preceding quotation is that human freedoms are an entitlement which all human beings need to enjoy. Sadly, most men and women in Africa are denied their right to various freedoms because of factors such as culture, tradition, or just the total lack of democracy. As Okri further states, we need to "question everything, in order to rebuild for the future . . . and redream the world" (ibid: 132).[1]

While Okri's words are an exhortation to every individual to reflect on and rethink the circumstances of his or her life, they are particularly pertinent to intellectuals – individuals who have the knack of understanding their mission in life as one which involves "redreaming the world". The words sound a salutary note about the need for intellectuals to envision a world in which all people are able to relish and revel in the values of freedom and equality. The words are a salutary reminder of the challenges which a black African intellectual will have to face up to in the twenty-first century. The challenges are particularly daunting in the wake of a continent

76 *A paradigm of an African intellectual*

whose majority population has not only emerged from the claws of colonialism in the last fifty years but also has individuals who want to retain the hold on tradition to which most (black) African people are quite susceptible. It is difficult to imagine how intellectuals will deal with the dilemma which involves notions of tradition, culture, and heritage pulling them in one direction and the imperative to be global citizens in another. Further, in the post-colonial, post-independence dispensation, intellectuals will have to grapple with challenges such as the lures of nationalism and power. In the changing world of the twenty-first century, it would be unfortunate to see a black African intellectual making, disseminating, and promoting smug assumptions about so-called African culture, as if the African continent is a monoculture, rather than striking a meaningful cultural middle ground in the changing world of the twenty-first century, where notions of culture and identity are always in a state of transition. Still more, other dilemmas for the intellectual to shun include yielding to the lures of nationalist sentiments and the power that such sentiments bring with them. This is because the African continent as we know it in the twenty-first century is not hermetically sealed from the rest of the world. We inhabit a world where foundations of what used to be perceived as absolute truths, regarding categories such as race, gender, sexuality, and class, have been thrown into question because the world is slowly embracing trendy, civilised, and refined ideas with regard to these notions. For instance, erstwhile so-called determinate ideologies, such as that of patriarchy, are now being rejected in Africa as more women are now given an opportunity to go to school. Thus, technological advances in the form of social media largely define identities in our time. The kinds of cultural inscriptions we see in schools, in our sitting rooms as we watch TV, and at the workplace, to mention a few examples, suggest that the continent is in a state of transition. The questions worth posing include the following: How do African intellectuals, to use Joseph Ki-zerbo's words, "develop an active neutrality, . . . a positive autonomy, as opposed to the one that is inert, amorphous and mute" (2005: 80)? In other words, how do we ensure that "African intellectuals have to be at the forefront of responsible citizenship" (ibid: 81)? Further, how do African intellectuals develop among the citizenry a spirit of non-partisanship to ensure that there is justice in society? This entails that, as champions of the conscience, African intellectuals should always show both the politicians and citizenry the link between ideas and social reality, especially how such a nexus points to notions of social justice.

The twenty-first century radically differs from the previous ones – centuries which were largely influenced by all manner of excesses, in particular the one about colonialism. But, with the end of colonialism, most African problems are multiple and somewhat different, and these include ethnic conflicts and the lack of democracy and other freedoms, as well as the reality of migration not only within the continent but also to other parts of the world. Remarkably, as far as migration is concerned, in recent times, such movements have led to all forms of excesses among black people, including instances of xenophobia and child trafficking, as well as deaths in the Mediterranean Sea as a number of black people leave the African continent for Europe in search of better lives. This is largely because of poor governance, religious extremism, and intolerance in most African countries. Clearly, these are instances of a continent of fractured identities where most black people fail to live with one another in harmony, because most of the political leaders wallow in the cult of personality or simply because of their Machiavellian approach to power and governance which makes them believe in the force of nationalism. In a technologically mediated world, such as the twenty-first century, very few politicians realise that the issue of nationalism has to be looked at anew. Therefore, the complexion and complexities of the challenges that the African intellectual has to grapple with are, to all intents and purposes, of cosmopolitan cultures, meaning they are all-inclusive and global. With a few exceptions, post-colonial Africa has gone through all manner of crises, including dictatorships, ethnic conflicts, a lack of democratic values, a denial of human rights, economic stagnation, and corruption, to mention some examples. Other persistent problems include all forms of discrimination in society, especially ones based on gender, sexuality, and ethnicity. All these problems persist on a continent where the perennial ills of ignorance, hunger, and disease also prevail in most societies. This state of affairs puts enormous demands on the African intellectual. There is a need for a type of African intellectual who, to use either Gramsci's or Edward Said's term, is an "organic" intellectual – somebody who is prepared to give voice to such pressing challenges in society by "speaking the truth to power", to use Said's famous expression. Such an intellectual must resist the temptation to align himself or herself with the ruling elites. Instead, she or he must be the kind of individual who uses knowledge and skills to advance the humanities for the betterment of humankind. This means that, as well as being guardians of democracy, African intellectuals need to be at the forefront of protecting various kinds of rights and freedoms.

Paragons of African/Africanist intellectualism

Philosophy

Firstly, as far as philosophy is concerned, particularly one which deals with the contentious issue of what is seen as the world civilisation, Cheick Anta Diop remains one of the most prominent black African intellectuals to have emerged in Africa in the second half of the twentieth century. In

78 *A paradigm of an African intellectual*

his famous text *The African Origin of Civilization: Myth or Reality*, Diop made a case for the fact that what was called Egyptian civilisation was of black (Negro) origin. This explains why he went on to argue that what is known as Western civilisation was not Eurocentric in nature because, just as the Romans learnt from the Greeks, the Greeks themselves learnt from the black Egyptians. While some scholars do not agree with Diop on this issue, what makes him stand out as a typical African intellectual is the fact that his approach to undertaking research was objective and non-partisan. It is easy to appreciate Diop's logic (that the so-called Western civilisation is not wholly Eurocentric), because when one thinks about the reality of Christianity, which became part of the Enlightenment modernity before being embraced globally, one appreciates this religion's Semitic origins. Further, in terms of arithmetic language and practice, according to which we learn about both Roman and Arabic numerals, what some scholars see as being solely Eurocentric knowledge is not exclusively European. For Diop, most knowledge is universal and multicultural. This explains why Anthony Appiah has argued that Diop saw "the importance of ancient Egyptian philosophy for the contemporary African intellectual life" (1992: 101).

Politics

Secondly, in Julien Benda's sense of seeing an intellectual as being located in the category of a breed of individuals in society who question certainties, Nelson Mandela stands out as a paradigm of such intellectuals. As will become evident, Mandela also fits the bill with regard to the ideas of scholars such as Antonio Gramsci, Edward Said, and Julia Kristeva, the first two having adapted Julien Benda's notions and understanding of the concept of an *intellectual (or a clerk)*. This is because Mandela's personal philosophy and creed, which find articulation in his famous "I Am Prepared to Die" speech – the speech he gave during his treason trial in 1964 – attests to the type of individual whose true merit lies in being part of humanity. In a word, for Mandela, the idea of humanity transcends racial and other divisions, and hence, he had digested, with admirable clarity, the fact that culture is a site of values which transcend any form of particularism in the form of race. In his speech, it is clear that all notions of his personal identity became manifest – the kind of identity in which a great deal of emphasis is placed on community, morality, and justice. The Rivonia trial stands out as the most pulsating example in which Mandela emerges as an intellectual par excellence. Fitting into Gramsci's idea of an "organic" mould of an intellectual, Mandela says,

> South Africa is the richest country in Africa, and could be one of the richest countries in the world. But it is a land of extremes and remark-

A paradigm of an African intellectual 79

able contrasts. The whites enjoy what may well be the highest standard of living in the world, whilst Africans live in poverty and misery.

(1964: 271)

This quotation eloquently points to Mandela's ability to pinpoint problems in his society, seeing justice as the noblest ideal to introduce into a society which was polarised on the basis of race. As an intellectual, he simply did not want to see and live in such a lopsided society.

Later, in a statement of his defence at the Rivonia trial, Mandela demonstrates that he is an intellectual who is there to serve political interests and further the cause of justice. He states that

> [d]uring my lifetime I have dedicated myself to this struggle of the African people. I have fought against white domination, and I have fought against black domination. I have cherished the ideal of a democratic and free society in which all persons live together in harmony and with equal opportunities. It is an ideal which I hope to live for and achieve. But if needs be, it an ideal for which I am prepared to die.

(ibid: 273)

As a political activist, Mandela's entire speech during his trial goes to the heart of the debate about the kind of intellectual that he is, and this explains why the two preceding quotations particularly demonstrate the extent to which his fame came to rest on his convictions – the kind of convictions which underscore the importance of a common humanity. Here is an individual who refuses to be beholden to power. If, as they say, intellectuals are the kinds of thinkers or critics who are seen as attending seriously to life and not escaping from it, then the appellation *intellectual* fits Mandela perfectly since he does not totalise experience. Instead, questions of dogma and orthodoxy, which were built into the politics of his day in South Africa, enabled him to pointedly highlight and pinpoint crucial problems in his society, seeing justice as the noblest ideal to aspire to and live for. Thus, by dedicating his life to working for racial harmony and peace, he embodies the spirit of intellectualism for which he will be remembered for millennia. Even though, across the African continent, there were other "political" intellectuals who were called "pioneering politicians", such as Kwame Nkrumah, Julius Nyerere, and Kenneth Kaunda, to mention a few examples, and ensured that most of the African continent became independent from colonial rule, as an intellectual, Mandela will be remembered because, rather than embrace nativism (which most black leaders of his generation did), he believed in and promoted the intersubjective realm of culture and identity according to which various races can co-exist in perfect harmony.

80   *A paradigm of an African intellectual*

Writers of fiction

Apart from "political" intellectuals, such as Mandela, South Africa under apartheid also produced a great number of intellectuals in the form writers of fiction. This intellectual capital, to use Pierre Bourdieu's expression, produced fictional works which portrayed the damaging and reprehensible conditions lived by black people under the apartheid regime. It is these works which brought what was happening within South Africa to the attention of the outside world, drawing pungent criticism about the evils and depravity of apartheid. Among others, some of the well-known intellectuals of this type were Alan Paton, Richard Rive, Athol Fugard, Nadine Gordimer, Njabulo Ndebele, Bessie Head, and Ezekiel Mphahlele, to name a few examples. Of course, works of fiction by black writers, notably *Down Second Avenue* (by Eskia Mphahlele) and *Blame Me on History* (by Bloke Modisane), were representations of the ways in which South Africa, under apartheid, existed to debase black humanity. But at the same time, there were white writers, such as Alan Paton, Athol Fugard, and Nadine Gordimer who produced the kind of fiction whose threads or themes were no different from those of the black writers. For example, in Alan Paton's famous novel *Cry, the Beloved Country*, Paton showed the extent to which most South African lives had been wrecked by apartheid. As a believer of liberalism, Paton demonstrated his humanitarian line of thinking in his novel. Then, Athol Fugard's famous Elizabethan plays, including *Sizwe Bansi Is Dead*, were so interesting in that he was able to give depictions of the strains and tribulations of living in a country which had been ravaged by racial divisions of apartheid. Further, most of the fiction by Nadine Gordimer also testified to the struggles and suffering of living in a society which had been riven by racial conflicts. Thus, it was not surprising that, at one point in time, Gordimer was "regarded internationally as the literary conscience of South Africa" (Chapman 1996: 236).

To the extent that their works of fiction were a sore point to the apartheid government, writers of this distinctive feature were indeed intellectuals in the sense that some of them risked imprisonment or banishment for their writings. As Edward Said has put it, intellectuals "have to be thoroughgoing individuals with powerful personalities, and, above all, have to be in a state of almost permanent opposition to the status quo" (1994: 380). Thus, all of the aforementioned intellectuals were men and women who demonstrated their individuality, intellectual capacity and ingenuity through their fictional writings, even if they did so at a great risk to their lives.

Further, Nigerian writer of fiction and Nobel Peace Prize laureate Wole Soyinka remains another scintillating example of an "ivory tower" intellectual whose role was not restricted to knowledge production in the academe.

A paradigm of an African intellectual   81

Through his fiction and other writings, he will be remembered for weighing in on all forms of discourses on culture and African identity, as well as exposing the corruption and ineptitude of successive military regimes in his home country of Nigeria. For speaking out against political abuses, Soyinka had several confrontations with many military regimes and was subjected to all forms of harassment, including imprisonment. Further, as far as African cultural identity is concerned, the high-water mark of the Negritude movement saw Soyinka make a penetrating comment in the expression he would use in speeches, namely "a tiger doesn't have to proclaim its tigritude". Here, he was poking fun at those who were obsessed with the notion of African (black) identity and personality when real identity is about lived experience. Still on the idea of the Negritude, Soyinka remarked that

> [t]he final proof of negro humanity is in the human variety of its individuals, and the proof of negro maturity is his unhysterical acceptance of himself. Dignity, for me, has always been a quality incapable of being forced. The louder it is the more ludicrous the object becomes. The whole concept of negritude is, for this reason, particularly false. . . . The African personality is several and any attempt to straightjacket him is a travesty of his humanity.
>
> (quoted in Lindfors 2008: 58)

Soyinka here challenges the idea of the Negritude according to which the idea of African identity was presented as being based on the notion of racial blackness. He says the idea is "false" because he believes in the reality of Africa as being a web of a profoundly intertwined histories and memories – indigenous people such as the Khoisan (or Bushmen), Malays, the majority blacks, whites, Indians, Arabs, and other races.

Another African writer of fiction, a typical intellectual whose work questioned the social order of biopolitics, was Bessie Head. Although her career as a writer of fiction took off when she was a resident of South Africa at the height of apartheid, she became a writer of great renown when she emigrated to Botswana, where she wrote a lot of fiction in which she tacked a multiplicity of issues grounded in notions of essentialism, notably racism and patriarchy, which those who wield power in society are prone to champion. In her famous novel *A Question of Power*, Head not only exposes the ravaging effect of apartheid but also asks the question of what it means to be human on an African continent of exclusions based on race, gender, ethnicity, and other classifications. Thus, as a work of fiction which challenges the idea of biopolitics – the link between life and power – Head's text deconstructs the various dogmas which are built into ideas such as race, gender, ethnicity, heterosexuality, and religion. In this novel, apart from pinpointing the theme of racism, the main character goes on

82   *A paradigm of an African intellectual*

to identify and challenge all patriarchal structures and power hierarchies in societies which are real causes of pain and suffering for a great number of people. Further, all metaphysical forms of knowledge, such as religion, are also examined against a background of what is veritable and can be termed the truth. Head was a typically great African intellectual.

On the African continent, since the mid-1990s to date, the kind of intellectuals who have emerged as writers of fiction do not subscribe to the idea of a pure African identity. In fact, most of the works are "shaped more distinctly by contemporary notions of cosmopolitanism, globalisation, nomadism, and liminality" (Krishnan 2013: 74). Madhu Krishnan goes to state that the

> third generation African writers . . . portrays them as shaped more distinctly by contemporary notions of cosmopolitanism, globalization, nomadism, and liminality than their predecessors. Positioned in this postmodern milieu, third generation writers have been heralded for their questioning of over-determined identity markers and their deconstruction of totalities such as history, nation, gender, and their representative symbologies . . . , mirroring a larger global tendency in the postcolonial and African novel to embrace what has been called the "migration of memory" and "traveling identities".
>
> (ibid: 74)

In other words, the third generation of African literature is the kind of fiction which challenges all transcendent notions of cultural holism or purity, presenting the idea of cultural identity as a dynamic and fluid category. Some of the works include Nurudin Farah's *Knots*, which deals with the idea of an African state as largely a failed state. Other works which deal with the various themes Krishnan has listed include Kopano Matlwa's *Coconut*, Nonviolet Bulawayo's *We Need New Names*, J. M. Coetzee's *Diary of a Bad Year*, and Binyavanga Wainaina's *One Day I Will Write About This Place*.

Social activists

Botswana – probably a known beacon of democratic values in Africa – has produced one of the most forthright and outstanding public intellectuals in Southern Africa. A writer of fiction, as well as a committed social and political activist in her country of Botswana, Unity Dow will be remembered for standing up to the universal institution of patriarchy – a non-racial institution which has been the source of suffering for women across cultures. As an intellectual with a combative spirit, Dow challenged what were clearly asymmetries of power between men and women in her country of

A paradigm of an African intellectual 83

Botswana, where women's rights were not recognised. Having received her education and training in law, this truly remarkable woman would fight a gender ideology in her country which had confined women and children to the status of second-class citizens before the law – a law which pandered to patriarchal whims and the force of tradition. As she has argued, "Botswana as a whole, whether it be general or customary law, is overwhelmingly patriarchal in nature, upholding the supremacy and leadership of the male gender" (Dow et al. 1997: 459). Unity Dow was able to expose the sexist nature of the Botswana law in 1990. Having married a foreign white man who was domiciled in his wife's country (of Botswana), Dow realised that, while Botswana men could marry foreign women and their children would become Botswana citizens, children born in matrimonial relationships between Botswana women and foreign men would not be allowed to become Botswana citizens. According to the law, women who married men of foreign nationalities were seen as threatening and undermining the purity and stability of Botswana cultural traditions – hence identity. So, democracy, in all its manifestations did not apply to women. As a Botswana high court judge at the time, Dow took her government to court over citizenship laws that demonstrably discriminated against women and children. As I have put it elsewhere,

> What followed was a protracted legal battle lasting approximately four years. . . . In a court judgement that was delivered in 1994, and seen as a real challenge to male hegemony Unity Dow won the case, the judgment basing its evidence not on epistemological yet spurious and specious notions of African or Botswana culture, but rather on international conventions of which the postcolonial nation of Botswana was and still is a signatory.
>
> (Kalua 2010: 84)

This landmark ruling or judgement not only jolted the Botswana male fraternity out of its complacency with regard to matters of culture and tradition but also meant that Dow had achieved gender parity for Botswana women using the legal framework. Through this case, Dow had participated in the trashing of any vestiges of tradition which were built into the statute which was clearly the bastion of male chauvinism and dominance.

Further, looking at the issue of women's empowerment in general, Dow et al. have this to say:

> [w]omen, especially hard-hit by inequities in all spheres of public and private life, have been identified as a priority for educational programs to improve their opportunities for increased participation in the civil

84   *A paradigm of an African intellectual*

and political realm as well as economic, social and cultural arenas of their respective nations.

(1997: 455)

In 2001, Dow would write a thought-provoking paper in which she opines about the unfortunate destiny of African women. Entitled "How the Global Informs the Local: The Botswana Citizenship Case", Dow states,

> First, that women in Africa have not been involved in the formulation and/or interpretation and/or implementation of what are now accepted norms and concepts that inform current notions of human rights, democracy, and good governance. Second, women's contact with systems that are traditionally viewed as the bedrock of democracy and good governance have been from a position of weakness, in roles of servants, objects, and exceptions to the general rule. Third, women have not been participants, on an equal basis with men, in the negotiation, formulation, development, and implementation of national constitutions. Fourth, many national constitutions fail to guarantee women rights with men under the law. Fifth, I suggest, that only when women are equal actors in the process can there be a legitimate claim that Africa is on the road to democracy. Finally, the local cannot remain isolated and exclusively self-informing, and, consequently, the global must inform and influence the local.

(2001: 319)

Unity Dow's major concerns are the lack of women's involvement in many domains of life, precisely as a result of multiple constraints imposed on them by the dictates of patriarchy or male chauvinism. Here, Dow is demonstrating what a treasure trove of ideas she is by articulating a vision of shifting post-colonial identities in which the global has some influence over the local and the local incrementally becomes a hybrid by drawing on the global. Thus, by holding up a mirror to African cultures' flaws in the face of modernity, Dow is an ideal intellectual who is prepared to contribute to change and transformation in her society. She is an intellectual who will be remembered for shedding light on the various forms of transitions that her society is going through. Further, as a writer of fiction, Dow wrote novels such as *The Screaming of the Innocent*, *Juggling Truths*, and *The Heavens May Fall*, which foreground the pervasiveness of tradition in her society where the overbearing institution of patriarchy makes life for women not worth living. Yet again, because Botswana is a rich African country, Dow's fiction introduces the kinds of representations of the country as a new template of transformation which has been brought about by modernisation so

A paradigm of an African intellectual 85

that, gradually, quite a number of people do enjoy the reality of borderlands of cultures.

Finally, in the second decade of the twenty-first century, South Africa would see its own public intellectual in the name of Thuli Madonsela – the country's public protector between 2009 and the end of her tenure in 2016. Edward Said has argued that "organic" intellectuals of the Gramscian mould are "pivotal to the workings of modern society" (2003: 383), and Madonsela fits the bill of an intellectual who is prepared to remind politicians about the value of being attuned to the needs of the populace, rather than being totally removed from day-to-day reality. As a mandarin, or public servant who went about her job with self-assurance and equanimity, this powerful woman's affirmation of her own intellectual freedom was exemplified or rendered visible in the way she dealt with some high-profile cases in which she challenged Jacob Zuma's presidency for all manner of excesses. Seeing that President Zuma's private ambitions were mixed poisonously with politics – the latter being a calling which demands that one serves one's people – Madonsela was the type of intellectual with a measured perspective on things, who always tried to get to the bottom of issues, rather than skim over them. As Michel Foucault has observed, "[i]t is necessary to think of the political problems of intellectuals . . . in terms of truth and power" (2001: 318). To that end, Madonsela, as Foucault further put it, represents the type of intellectual who "can operate and struggle at the general level of that regime of truth which is so essential to the structure and functioning of our society" (ibid: 318). In other words, as a public intellectual at a time when allegations of corruption in government circles were rife, she did not just abandon herself to a state of insouciant indifference. Instead, her true persona as a public intellectual was revealed in her skill, daring, and ability to lift a lid on all forms of rackets and related government abuses of power. Thus, as public protector, Madonsela would build "a reputation as a fearless watchdog . . . after her appointment in 2009" (De Wet 2016: 1). Without a shred of compromise, she went on to produce a report in which the goings-on involving former President Zuma's acts of corruption were laid bare. What Madonsela brought out into the open with regard to Nkandla (or Zuma's village) were all manner of lies, distortions, and obfuscation emerging from the collusion between the president, politicians, and government officials. For example, in the second report, dubbed the notorious "state capture" report, Madonsela was able to expose the way in which Zuma had found himself prone to all forms of manipulation by powerful people in society. For example, she exposed Mr Ajay Gupta, President Zuma's close ally, with regard to the way he had some political influence as far as the issue of the president giving people ministerial portfolios was concerned. Thus there were

86 *A paradigm of an African intellectual*

allegations that his family appeared to have the power to hire and fire Cabinet ministers and board members of state-owned enterprises to score lucrative government deals.

(Van Wyk et al. 2016: 1)

Madonsela states that such abuses of political power came to light through

breaches of the executive ethics code by Zuma, allegedly enabling the Guptas to offer ministerial positions on his behalf.

(ibid: 2)

Madonsela's charisma is characteristic of what Kristeva has termed the intellectual dissident in that she was able to check and break the grip on power of President Zuma and other political elites whose exercise of hegemony was gradually destroying the democratic foundation on which the South African nation-state is based. She is a typical intellectual whom society needs in order to make substantive progress because she wears the mantle of authority which allows her to take perceptive assessments of situations which relate to governance and impact the public. As Noam Chomsky has put it, "[i]t is the responsibility of intellectuals to speak the truth and expose lies" (1967: 2). In other words, there is a tendency of obfuscation and distortion in political circles, and it is the duty of the intellectual to conscientise the public about political transgression and wrongdoing by those who wield political power. As the South African public protector, Thuli Madonsela was able to pinpoint all forms of lies and obfuscation by those who wielded power during Jacob Zuma's presidency. To the extent that she was able to transform public discourses in ways which are perceived as notable humanistic interventions in society, Madonsela stands out as a model of an "organic" African intellectual whom other black African intellectuals need to emulate if they are to transform the continent in the twenty-first century.

Chapter summary

A paradigm of African intellectuals in the twenty-first century entails having particular individuals whose distinguishing attributes point to the ability to be knowledgeable about a great deal of issues in society, including domains of knowledge such as politics, ideology, culture, race, ethnicity, gender, sexuality, religion and many other categorisations which are located in the sphere of knowledge production and identity issues. African intellectuals need to develop a deep awareness and understanding of the nature of particular forms of knowledge which drive society forward.

Note

1 For Okri, learning to embrace freedom requires that we question forms of truth and reality which make claims to some transcendence.

Conclusion

Throughout this primer, I have pinpointed the role of a model "organic" intellectual – an endowed individual who comes up with forms of critique or constructive criticism which reject outright particular forms of political interests and cultural formations which deny some people a right to full humanity. To that end, I have offered differing delineations of the concept of intellectual, demonstrating how vague and indeterminate it is, largely because the idea emerged in the Renaissance period, even though it has been a trans-historical notion because great thinkers have been part of most societies. I have presented the idea of an intellectual as conceived and theorised by various scholars and have demonstrated the extent to which the concept of an intellectual is value-laden and open to several interpretations. This became clear as I looked at the various ways in which the word *intellectual* has been posited and theorised by various scholars. For this reason, I have attempted to clearly unpack and fully contextualise the notion of an intellectual from various perspectives and understandings, going back to the Greek period, the first century AD, the Middle Ages, the Renaissance, and the Enlightenment. For example, I have traced the nature and role of African intellectuals going back to the colonial, pre-independence era, up until the first two decades of the twenty-first century. I have done so in order to gain a vantage point from which to pinpoint and reimagine the type of African public intellectuals who would make a difference in their societies in the twenty-first century. In the end, I have attempted to fully frame a broad paradigm of who an African intellectual is and how she or he should learn to grapple with current dilemmas (in Africa) which are commensurate to those other African intellectuals have had to contend with in the last fifty years or so since the end of colonialism.

On the African continent, I have contextualised the post-colonial, post-independence Africa, making it clear that most leading African intellectuals were associated with the struggle against colonialism, but once independence had been attained in most African countries, a good number of these

88 *Conclusion*

intellectuals who served the "political" cause through co-option were conflicted about issues such as democracy and nationalism. Most of these politicians were products of so-called liberation movements in Africa, which later morphed into political parties. Thus, one has seen one-party states dressed up as democracies through the manipulation of their electorate and the elections. I have consistently argued that the African continent needs "organic" intellectuals. On this continent, sometimes the law is used to serve some individuals and protect vested interests. Moreover, society is always rocked by social ills, such as illiteracy, disease, hunger, crime, and corruption. Thus "organic" intellectuals are a must-have group of people in society. As Edward Said has argued, since they "traffic in ideas" (1991: 80), they should be seen as "playing the important role of gaining legitimacy and currency of ideas" (ibid: 80). Further, intellectuals "are never more themselves than when, moved by metaphysical passion and disinterred principles of justice and truth, they denounce corruption, defend the weak, defy imperfect or oppressive authority" (Said 1994: 380). In other words, as discerning members of society, as well as great thinkers of the brave new world of the twenty-first century, intellectuals should address some of the thorny problems besetting post-colonial Africa in the realms of race, ethnicity, gender, religion, nationality, and other related categories. As the bulwark against all forms of radicalism, intellectuals should openly attack the bungling incompetence of some African politicians who take advantage of the largely blinkered populations to stay in power for years on end. On a continent where politics infuses the lives of many politicians, intellectuals must be primed to fight particular trends in society, notably dictatorship, patriarchy, ethnic conflict, and other tendencies which threaten the very fabric of society.

Within the Southern African region and context, instances of the delimited nature of the concept of an intellectual have been proffered, ranging widely from those who fought against colonial oppression to those who are both specific and largely universal intellectuals, such as Nelson Mandela, who embodied the values of humanity. Further, I have mentioned, albeit in passing, other instances of intellectuals who have existed to conscientise the public, notably writers of fiction such as Alan Paton, Nadine Gordimer, and Njabulo Ndebele, as well as political and social activists who worked hard to raise people's awareness about the scourge of apartheid. I have also alluded to specific intellectuals who refuse to cater to power, notably former top South African civil servant Thuli Madonsela, who, as the South African government's public protector, remained an intellectual par excellence in her ability to reflect the kinds of interventions which are at the service of values such as democracy, fairness, and human rights. Finally, in the instance of Botswana, Unity Dow stands out as one of the most exemplary

Conclusion 89

of intellectuals through her activism, as well as her fight for the rights of women and children. By pinpointing gender inequality that was embedded in the Botswana constitution and only served the interests of patriarchal power, Dow remains a typically "organic" intellectual. For both Dow and Madonsela, by articulating the idea of human rights and through their interventions in issues of culture and social justice respectively, they are consummate examples of genuine intellectuals and epitomise true models of what black African intellectuals should be like if they are to best serve the continent and the world in the twenty-first century.

All in all, I have also contextualised the idea of an African intellectual who may be a politician, an academic, a cosmopolitan scholar, or any individual who is specially endowed to defend a cause, as well as see through the incompetence and chicaneries of political leaders and expose corruption amongst the ruling elites. In short, Africa needs the kind of intellectuals who will champion the cause of justice on a continent which has always been afflicted and riven by all manner of conflicts, including ethnic wars and cleansing, as well genocides. For Henry Giroux, "the role of an intellectual is the struggle for social change" (2002: 386). My main argument in this monograph is that we need black African intellectuals who are typically engaged public thinkers in that they make a difference by trying to nurture public discourses in ways which will promote change in society. Like Mandela, an intellectual must confront and challenge (rather than uncritically embrace) dogma or orthodoxy. An intellectual should fight against determinism, comment on the prevailing political configuration of our world, and demonstrate the responsibility of broadening horizons for the public or citizenry when it comes to issues such as politics, culture, and identity. There is a need for intellectuals to adhere to ethics of responsibility as world citizens. An intellectual is somebody who has developed a great awareness of the importance of caring deeply about values which make us all human.

Works cited

Ahluwalia, P. 2010. *Out of Africa: Post-Structuralism's Colonial Roots*. London & New York: Routledge.

Appiah, A.A. 1992. *In My Father's House: Africa in the Philosophy of Culture*. New York & Oxford: Oxford University Press.

Barber, B. 1998. *Intellectuals Pursuits: Toward an Understanding of Culture*. New York & Oxford: Rowman & Littlefield Publishers, Inc.

Benda, J. 1955. *The Betrayal of the Intellectuals (La Trahison Des Clercs)*. Translated by Richard Aldington. Boston, MA: The Beacon Press.

Bgoya, W. 2014. '50 Years of Independence: Reflections on the Role of Publishing and Progressive African Intellectuals', *Africa Spectrum*, 49 (13): 107–119.

Bhabha, H.K. 2004. *The Location of Culture*. London & New York: Routledge.

Castle, G. 2007. *The Blackwell Guide to Literary Theory*. Malden & Oxford: Blackwell Publishing.

Chapman, M. 1996. *Southern African Literatures*. London & New York: Longman.

Charle, C. (ed.). 2015. *Birth of Intellectuals: 1800–1900*. Cambridge & Malden, MA: Polity Press.

Cheah, P. 2016. *What is a World? On Postcolonial Literatures as World Literature*. Durham & London: Duke University Press.

Chomsky, N. 1967. 'The Responsibilities of Intellectuals', *The New York Review of Books*, February 23, 1967, pp. 2–23.

Chomsky, N. 1978. *Intellectuals and the State*. Vertaling: Gerda Telgenhof.

Collini, S. 2006. *Absent Minds: Intellectuals in Britain*. Oxford & New York: Oxford University Press.

Creary, N.M. 2012. *African Intellectuals and Decolonization*. Athens: Ohio University Press.

Danielsson, S.K. 2005. 'The Intellectual as an Architect and Legitimizer of Genocide: Benda Redux', *Journal of Genocide Research*, 7 (3): 393–407.

De Wet, P. 2016. 'Public Protector's Big Shoes Await', *Mail and Guardian*, August 12, 2016, pp. 8–12.

Demers, D. 2011. *The Ivory Tower of Babel: Why the Social Sciences Are Failing to Live Up to Their Promises*. New York: Algora Publishing.

Diop, C.A. 1974. *The African Origin of Civilization: Myth or Reality?* New York & Westport, CT: Lawrence Hill and Company.

Works cited 91

Distiller, N. 2012. *Shakespeare and the Coconuts: On Post-apartheid South African Culture*. Johannesburg: Wits University Press.

Dow, U. 2001. 'How the Global Informs the Local: the Botswana Citizenship Case', *Healthcare for Women* (22): 319–331.

Dow, U., Stumbras, S. & Tutten, S. 1997. 'Looking at Women's Empowerment Initiatives from a Grassroots Level', in *Human Rights Education for the Twenty-first Century*, edited by G.J. Andrepoulos & R.P. Claude (pp. 455–468). Philadelphia: University of Pennsylvania Press.

Fleming, T.K. 2016. 'From One Colonial Situation to Another: Politics, Universalism and the Crisis of the African Intellectual', *Africology: The Journal of African Studies*, 9 (4): 289–317.

Foucault, M. 2001. 'Truth and Power', in *The Nature of Truth: Classic and Contemporary Perspectives*, edited by Michal Lynch (pp. 317–319). Cambridge, MA: MIT Press.

Gardner, S. 1992. *Red Vienna and the Golden Age of Psychology, 1918–1938*. New York & London: Praeger.

Giroux, H.A. 2002. 'Public Intellectuals, Race and Public Space', in *A Companion to Racial and Ethnic Studies*, edited by David Theo Goldberg & John Solomons (pp. 383–404). Malden & Oxford: Blackwell Publishers.

Gramsci, A. 1996. 'The Intellectuals' (from Prison Notebooks)', in *The Continental Philosopher Reader*, edited by Richard Kearney & Mara Rainwater (pp. 184–193). London & New York: Routledge.

Grosfoguel, R. 2012. Decolonizing Western Uni-versalisms: Decolonial Pluriversalism from Aime Cesaire to the Zapatistas', *Transmodernity: Journal of Peripheral Cultural Production of the Luso-Hispanic World*, 1 (3): 88–104.

Holman Christian Standard Bible. 2003. Nashville: Holman Bible Publishers.

Isasi-Diaz, A.M. & Mendieta, E. 2012. *Decolonizing Epistemologies: Latina/o Theology and Philosophy*. New York: Fordham University Press.

Jacoby, R. 1987. *The Last Intellectuals: American Culture in the Age of Academe*. New York: Basic Books.

Kalua, F.A. 2010. 'Identities in Transition: The 1990 High Court Case and Unity Dow's The Heavens May Fall', *Journal of Literary Studies*, 26 (2): 80–89.

Ki-zerbo, J. 2005. 'African Intellectuals, Nationalism, and Pan-Africanism: A Testimony', in 'African Intellectuals and Nationalism', in *African Intellectuals: Rethinking Politics, Gender and Development* (pp. 78–93). New York, London & Pretoria: Zed Books Ltd & Unisa Press.

Krishnan, M. 2013. 'Affiliation, Disavowal, and National Commitment in Third Generation of African Literature', *Ariel: A Review of International English Literature*, 44 (1): 73–97.

Kristeva, J. 1986. 'A New Type of Intellectual: The Dissident', in *The Kristeva Reader*, edited by Toril Moi (pp. 292–300). New York: Columbia University Press.

Lindfors, B. 2008. *Early Soyinka*. Trenton and Asmara: Africa World Press.

Mandela, N. 1964. 'I am Prepared to Die', http:www.anc.org.za/ansdocs/history/Mandela/1960/rivonia.html

Mandela, N. 2010. 'I am Prepared to Die', in *Leadership: Essential Selections on Power, Authority, and Influence*, edited and with commentary by Barbara Kellerman (pp. 264–275). New York & London: McGraw Hill.

92 Works cited

Marzagora, S. 2016. 'The Humanism of Reconstruction: African Intellectuals, Decolonial Critical Theory, and the Opposition to 'Posts' (Postmodernism, Poststructuralism and Postcolonialism)', *Journal of Cultural Studies*, 28 (2): 161–178.

Mbeki, T. 1998. *Africa, the Time Has Come (Selected Speeches)*. Cape Town: Tafelberg Publishers Ltd & Mafube Publishing.

McLennan, G. 2013. 'Postcolonial Critique: The Necessity of Sociology', *Political Power and Social Theory*, 24 (1): 119–144.

Mistry, J. 2001. 'Conditions of Cultural Production in Post-apartheid South Africa', in *IWM Junior Visiting Fellows Conferences*, vol. xi/8 (1): pp. 1–20.

Mkandawire, T. (ed.). 2005a. *African Intellectuals: Rethinking Politics, Gender and Development*. New York, London & Pretoria: Zed Books Ltd & Unisa Press.

Mkandawire, T. 2005b. 'African Intellectuals and Nationalism', in *African Intellectuals: Rethinking Politics, Gender and Development* (pp. 10–55). New York, London & Pretoria: Zed Books Ltd & Unisa Press.

Molnar, T. 1994. *The Decline of the Intellectual*. New Brunswick, NJ & London: Transaction Publishers.

Mphahlele, E. 1974. *The African Image*. New York: Praeger.

National Research Foundation of South Africa (NRF). 2015. 'NRF Rating', http://www.nrf.ac.za/rating

Nesbitt, F.N. 2003. 'African Intellectuals in the Belly of the Beast: Migration, Identity and the Politics of African Intellectuals in the North', *Critical Arts*, 1 & 2: 17–35.

Nesbitt, F.N. 2008. 'Post-colonial Anxieties: (Re)presenting African Intellectuals', *African Affairs*, 107 (427): 273–282.

Okri, B. 1997. *A Way of Being Free*. London: Phoenix House.

Parry, B. 1996. 'Resistance Theory/Theorizing Resistance or Two Cheers for Nativism', in *Contemporary Postcolonial Theory: A Reader*, edited by Padmin Mongia (pp. 84–109). New York: Arnold.

Plato, 1974. *Republic*. Introduced and translated by G. M. A. Grube, Indianapolis, IN: Hackett Publishing Company.

Reich, E. 1969. *Plato as an Introduction to Modern Criticism of Life*. London & Washington, DC: Kennikat Press.

Said, E.W. 1991. *The World, the Text and the Critic*. London: Vintage.

Said, E.W. 1994. *Representations of the Intellectual: The 1993 Reith Lectures*. New York: Pantheon.

Said, E.W. 2003. 'Representations of the Intellectual', in *Social Theory: Essential Readings*, edited and introduced by Gordon Bailey & Noga Gayle (pp. 379–388). Oxford & New York: Oxford University Press.

Van Wyk, P. Bezuidenhout, J. & Letsoalo, M. 2016. 'State Capture: Commission of Inquiry Wanted', *Mail and Guardian*. October 14, 2016, pp. 10–14.

Varadharajan, A. 2013. 'Edward Said and the (Mis)fortunes of the Public Intellectual', *College Literature: A Journal of Critical Literary Studies*, 40 (4): 52–73.

Index

Achebe, Chinua 58
Africa, termed as polysemy 25–26
African/Africanist intellectuals:
  apartheid period 25; Appiah
  view of 24, 25; colonialism and
  4–5, 27; culture and (*see* culture,
  Black African intellectuals and);
  decolonising knowledge and 60–64;
  definition of 4–5; described 3;
  during slavery era 26–27; evolution
  of 26–28; future, described 7; ivory
  tower, post-colonialism 33–36
  (*see also* African ivory tower
  intellectuals; dilemmas of post-
  colonialism African intellectuals);
  Mazrui as 25; Nesbitt definition
  24–25; philosophy and 77–78;
  politics and 78–79; post-colonial
  27; pre-colonial 26; race and
  9–10; social activists and 82–86;
  theorising 24–26; in twenty-
  first century (*see* twenty-first
  century African intellectuals); and
  Western intellectuals (*see* Western
  intellectuals); white writers of fiction
  as 25; writers of fiction and 80–82
African identity 24
*African Intellectuals and
  Decolonization* (Creary) 60
African ivory tower intellectuals:
  dilemmas of (*see* dilemmas of post-
  colonialism African intellectuals);
  post-colonialism 33–34; prophetic
  role of, in Africa 35–36
African National Congress of South
  Africa 39

Africanness, credo of 51
*African Origin of Civilization, The:
  Myth or Reality* (Diop) 62, 78
African Renaissance 52–57;
  challengers of 55–56
Afrocentricism 62
Animal Farm (Orwell) 73
Appiah, Anthony 58, 78; African/
  Africanist intellectuals, defining 24, 25
Armah, Ayi Kwei 48
Arnold, Matthew 57, 72

Beautiful Ones Are Not Yet Born, The
  (Armah) 48
Benda, Julien 27, 74; influence of, on
  Gramsci 19; intellectual concept of
  17–18, 78; model of intellectuals
  18; unique functions of intellectuals
  notion 20–21; Western intellectual
  and 68–69
Betrayal of the Intellectuals, The
  (Benda) 68–69
Bgoya, Walter 27–28, 33; dilemmas of
  African intellectuals and 41–42
Bhabha, Homi 58, 60
Bill Bryson's African Diary (Bryson) 73
blackness 50, 52
Black Skin, White Masks (Fanon) 62–63
Blame Me on History (Modisane) 80
Bourdieu, Pierre 35, 80
British Cultural Studies 72
Bryson, Bill 73
Bulawayo, Nonviolet 82

Cabral, Mical 33
Chakrabarty, Dipesh 60

94 *Index*

Charle, Christopher 2; intellectual concept, precursor to 15–16
Cheah, Pheng 61
Chomsky, Noam 2, 9, 27, 74, 86; value-oriented intellectuals 24; on Western intellectual 67–68
Coconut (Matlwa) 82
Coetzee, J. M. 82
Collini, S. 2; delineation of term intellectual 13–14
colonialism: African intellectual and 4–5; post- 33–34
co-option 38
Creary, Nicholas 60
Cry, the Beloved Country (Paton) 80
culture, Black African intellectuals and: African continent as monoculture and 51; African Renaissance and 52–57; Bhabha on 58, 59; decolonisation of knowledge and 59–64; defining 50; Distiller on 55–56; Giroux on 58–59; Marzagora on 50–51; Mbeki on 52–57; Mistry on 55; Negritude movement and 51–52; Parry on 52; perception of 57–59
Culture and Society 1750–1950 (Williams) 57

Danielsson, Sara 20–21, 69
decolonisation of knowledge: African/Africanist intellectuals and 60–64; Cheah on 61–62; culture and 59–64; Diop on 62; Fanon on 62–63; Khrishnan on 63; McLennan on 62
deconstruction, idea of 71–72
Demers, David 30
Derrida, Jacques 71–72
Devil on the Cross (Ngugi wa Thiong'o) 48
Diary of a Bad Year (Coetzee) 82
dilemmas of post-colonialism African intellectuals: Bgoya on 41–42; cheerleading for politicians as 41–47; Marzagora on 45; Mkandawire on 40–41, 42–43, 44, 45, 47; Nesbitt on 38, 39–40, 43–44, 46; reclaiming critical political roles 47–48; types of 38
Diop, Cheik Anta 62, 63, 77–78

discourse, idea of 71
discursive formations 70
Distiller, Natasha 55–56
Dow, Unity 82–85, 88–89
Down Second Avenue (Mphahlele) 80
Down Under (Bryson) 73
Du Bois, W. E. B. 26–27
Dussel, Enrique 59

epistemes 70

Fanon, Frantz 27, 60, 62–63
Farah, Nurudin 82
Fleming, Tracy 1
Foucault, Michel 74, 85; discourse on intellectuals 23, 71; linguistic turn and 70–71
Fugard, Athol 25, 27, 80

Gardner, Sheldon 32–33
Giroux, Henry 2, 89; commenting on Gramsci 20; on culture 58–59; on ivory tower intellectuals 34; public intellectual defined by 18
Gordimer, Nadine 25, 27, 80, 88
Gramsci, Antonio 2, 27, 78; intellectual concept of 18–20; "The Intellectuals" essay 19; traditional intellectuals 22; unique functions notion of 20
Greek intellectual(s) 16
Grosfoguel, Ramon 59; on decolonising knowledge 60
Gulliver's Travels (Swift) 73
Gupta, Ajay 85

Head, Bessie 80, 81–82
Heavens May Fall, The (Dow) 84
"How the Global Informs the Local: The Botswana Citizenship Case" (Dow) 84

"I Am an African" (Mbeki speech) 53
"I Am Prepared to Die" (Mandela speech) 78–79
"Intellectual as an Architect and Legitimizer of Genocide, The: Julien Benda Redux" (Danielsson) 69
intellectual concept, theorising: African/Africanist (*see* African/Africanist intellectuals); Benda

Index 95

context of 17–18, 19, 20–21; Charle
context of 15–16; Chomsky and
24; Collini definition/application
of 13–14; Danielsson and 20–21;
Foucault context of 23; Giroux and
18, 20; Gramsci insights into 18–20;
Jesus Christ and 16–17; Kristeva
context of 23–24; Molnar reflection
on 14–15; Plato and 16; Said
context of 21–23; Socrates and 16
intellectual dissidents 23–24
intellectual(s): African (*see* African/
Africanist intellectuals); in Bible
16–17; concept of, described 2–3, 6,
8–10 (*see also* intellectual concept,
theorising); definition of 2, 4–5;
Greek 16; ivory tower 6 (*see also*
ivory tower intellectuals); as "a man
of letters" 15–16; notion of word
5–8; organic 7–8, 9, 19, 22; political
41–47; pre-colonial 4–5; traditional
19, 20, 22; unique functions notion
of 20–21
"Intellectuals, The" (Gramsci) 19
ivory tower intellectuals: African,
post-colonialism 33–36; biblical
references to 30–31; Demers on
30; described 6; Gardner on 32–33;
Giroux on 34; history of 30–31;
universities and 31–33

Jesus Christ, as intellectual 16–17
Juggling Truths (Dow) 84

Kaunda, Kenneth 79
Khama, Seretse 47
Ki-zerbo, Joseph 76
Knots (Farah) 82
knowledge, decolonisation of: African/
Africanist intellectuals and 60–64;
Cheah on 61–62; culture and 59–64;
Diop on 62; Fanon on 62–63;
Khrishnan on 63; McLennan on 62
Krishnan, Madhu 63, 82
Kristeva, Julia 2, 27, 39, 78; intellectual
dissidents and 23–24

*La Trahison Des Clercs (The Betrayal
of the Intellectuals)* (Benda) 20
Lessing, Doris 27

linguistic turn 69–70
*Lost Continent, The: Travels in Small
Town America* (Bryson) 73

Madonsela, Thuli 85–86, 88
Mandela, Nelson 47, 78, 88
Manicheanism 27, 63
"man of letters" intellectual(s)
as 15–16
Marzagora, Sara 45; African culture
and 50–51
Matlwa, Kopano 82
Mazrui, Ali 9, 25
Mbeki, Thabo 52–57
McLennan, Gregory 62
Mignolo, Walter 59; on decolonising
knowledge 60
Mistry, Joyce 55
Mkandawire, Thandika, dilemmas of
African intellectuals and 40–41,
42–43, 44, 45, 47
Modisane, Bloke 80
Molnar, Thomas 2; reflection on
intellectual concept 14–15
Mphahlele, E. 27, 80; on Negritude
movement 52
Mugabe, Robert 46

nationalism 38, 62
National Research Foundation of South
Africa (NRF) 3
Ndebele, Njabulo 27, 80, 88
Negritude movement 51–52; Soyinka
and 81
Nesbitt, Francis: African/Africanist
intellectuals, defining 24–25;
comprador intelligentsia 43–44, 46;
on intellectuals leaving Africa 38,
39–40
Ngugi wa Thiong'o 48
Nkrumah, Kwame 79
Notes from a Small Island (Bryson) 73
Nyerere, Julius 79

Okri, Ben 75
One Day I Will Write About This Place
(Wainaina) 82
organic intellectuals 19, 77, 87–88;
Said and 7–8, 9, 22, 72–73, 85
Orwell, George 73

96 *Index*

Pan-Africanism 38–39, 45–46, 62
Parry, Benita 52
Paton, Alan 25, 27, 80, 88
philosophy, African/Africanist intellectualism and 77–78
pioneering politicians 39, 79
Plato 16
political intellectual(s) 41–47
politics, African/Africanist intellectualism and 78–79
post-colonial African intellectuals 27
post-colonialism: African ivory tower intellectuals and 33–34; dilemmas of, African intellectuals (*see* dilemmas of post-colonialism African intellectuals)
pre-colonial African intellectuals 26
Provincializing Europe (Chakrabarty) 60

Question of Power, A (Head) 81
Quijano, Anibal 59

race, African/Africanist intellectuals and 9–10
Reich, Emil 16
Rive, Richard 80

Said, Edward 2, 18, 27, 41, 66, 78, 88; context of intellectual concept 21–23; organic intellectual concept 7–8, 9, 22, 72–73, 85; as Palestinian intellectual 72–73; portrayal of intellectuals 6; on traditional intellectual concept 22
Screaming of the Innocent, The (Dow) 84
Short History of Nearly Everything, A (Bryson) 73
Sizwe Bansi Is Dead (Fugard) 80
slavery era, black intellectuals during 26–27

social activists, African/Africanist intellectualism and 82–86
Socrates 16
Soyinka, Wole 8, 80–81

Things Fall Apart (Achebe) 58
Torres, Nelson Maldonaldo 59
Toward the Decolonization of African Literature (Chinweiuzu, Jemie, and Madubuike) 62
traditional intellectual(s) 19, 20, 22, 68
twenty-first century African intellectuals: challenges facing 75–77; Ki-zerbo and 76; Okri and 75; overview of 75; philosophy and 77–78; politics and 78–79; social activists and 82–86; writers of fiction and 80–82

unique functions notion of intellectual(s) 20–21
universities as ivory towers 31–33

Wainaina, Binyavanga 82
We Need New Names (Bulawayo) 82
Western intellectuals: African intellectuals learning from 65–67, 73–74; Benda and 68–69; Bryson and 73; Chomsky and 67–68; Danielsson and 69; Derrida and 71–72; Foucault and 70–71; Gramsci and 68; linguistic turn movement and 69–70; Orwell and 73; Said and 72–73; Williams and 72
Williams, Raymond 57; culture idea and 72
writers of fiction, African/Africanist intellectualism and 80–82

Zuma, Jacob 85–86

Printed in the United States
by Baker & Taylor Publisher Services